Canyon County
A Treasure of Land & Its People

Published by:

Idaho PRESS-TRIBUNE
First thing *Every* morning!

James T. Barnes Jr. Publisher

ISBN 0-9704417-0-3

Printed by:
Caxton Printers, Ltd.

Printed in the United States

Cover photo:

No Time to Rest

Farming is hard work, with no coffee breaks.

Archie Diggs, in a typical irrigator's stance, leans on a shovel to rest on his farm in 1939 in the Bennett Community. Archie was born in the Bennett Community at the home of his parents, Lottie and Homer Diggs. He married Thelma Post in 1939 and bought the Urban Martineau property which his parents had rented 23 years before. They had two children and nine grandchildren.

Archie was a dedicated farmer and fond of animals. He even said he liked animals better than people. He won holiday yard decor contests, and he and his first wife, Thelma, were enthusiastic square dancers. The annual Bennett Community ice cream social was held at his home for several years.

After Thelma's death, Archie married Ethel Simon in 1960. In 1945 Archie moved to Nampa and barbered for eight years, and was part owner of Shelton-Diggs Barbershop on 12th Avenue where Ron's Clip Shop is now located.

Archie moved back to the farm in 1952 and farmed there until retirement in 1985 when he moved to Nampa with his second wife and raised flowers and luscious vegetables that he shared with family and friends.

From 1947 to 1954, Archie was a member of the Canyon County Sheriff's Posse, a life member of Nampa Elks Lodge, treasurer and volunteer of Upper Deer Flat Fire Department for 25 years, active member of the First United Presbyterian Church, Canyon County Pet Haven, and former member of Jaycees and Nampa Chamber of Commerce.

Archie died in 1996.

Photo submitted by Gladys Messer of Nampa

PREFACE

A message from the publisher:

This is our first venture into the book publishing arena, and we're pleased for several reasons.
We're pleased that you answered our call for historic photos. They all came from your private family
collections. To our knowledge, most of the photos in this book have not been published before.

We're pleased with the quantity and the quality of the photos you provided. There are more than 300
photos throughout the book, and on every page you'll find a historical gem.

And we're pleased that the book brought us into contact with so many of you. All in all, we looked at
more than 1,500 photos submitted from about 400 of you. We regret that we couldn't use them all in
this volume. It simply would have been too large.

Perhaps that will mean a Volume II in the future.

Meanwhile, we hope you enjoy Volume I of "Canyon County: A Treasure of Land and Its People."

As a newspaper, the Idaho Press-Tribune publishes a historical account of life on our side of the
valley each day. We enjoyed our venture into providing history in a different way. As I said, we are
pleased.

We hope you are pleased, too.

Jim Barnes

Jim Barnes
President and Publisher
Idaho Press-Tribune

ACKNOWLEDGEMENTS
Canyon County: A Treasure of Land and Its People
James T. Barnes Jr., Publisher

Idaho Press-Tribune Project Staff
Carolyn J. Sinnard, Executive Project Director
Shannon Borchert, Project Director and Book Editor
Denice L. King, Book Production and Cover Design
Laurinda Burch, Project Assistant
Toni Lepper, Project Assistant

Scanning, Layout and Technical Staff
Steven T. Julian, Technical Director
Shelly DeBoard
Stacy L. Hamilton
Denice L. King
D. Shalom Pennington

Editorial Support
Vickie Holbrook, Editorial Director
Lisa Evans
Marie Galyean
Kristin Rodine
Kaye Steffler
Jay Vail
Lora Volterk
Helen Warriner

Canyon County Historical Society
Pati Sweet
Wendy Miller

Hostetler's Grocery

The owners of H.H. Hostetler's grocery store in the Stockman Building on Main Street (now 1st Street) in Nampa pose for a picture in 1917. The two people at the left are unidentified. At the right are Herman Hostetler, Juanita Hostetler and Lyle.

Photo submitted by Vertie Hostetler Bailey of Nampa

Groundbreaking at Deer Flat Reservoir
Lake Lowell takes its name from J.H. Lowell, an irrigator who led the reclamation project to form the Payette-Boise Users' Association on March 4, 1904. Construction began in 1906. By 1911, it was finished. By then, there were nearly 3,000 farms that received irrigation water.
Photo submitted by Justine Gowen Hopper of Caldwell

Lake Machinery
After the groundbreaking, men working on the Lake Lowell project proudly display some of the machines used. *Photo submitted by Justine Gowen Hopper of Caldwell*

Farley Family Portrait

The W.W. Farley family gathers for a picture, typical of the style around 1901. The family came to the Parma area from Missouri in 1887 in a covered wagon. Farley and his wife homesteaded on a farm, where they raised their 13 children.
Photo submitted by Helen Mattox of Nampa

Olsen Family

Martin Olsen and his family are shown here on their farm on West Linden Street in Caldwell. He planted fruit trees and farmed, hauling fruit and produce to Silver City and DelMar. Martin immigrated to America from Norway in 1852 after being caught, and consequently escaping from, the Prussian Army. Olsen served as a cabin boy on a windjammer while making his way to America.
Photo submitted by Helen Olsen of Wilder

On the Bardsley Homestead

John L. Bardsley and wife Josie with their three children, Harriet, Charles and Homer, stand in front of their home where Lake Lowell is now. John L. worked hard for the dairy industry in Idaho and owned J.L. Bardsley and Co., an implement business.
Photo submitted by Shirley Simpson of Nampa

The Postman

This postman pauses in his appointed rounds as a College of Idaho student takes his picture on the college campus in Caldwell. The student sent the photo to fellow classmate Mrs. Lizzie Campbell in 1908.
Photo submitted by Don Johnson of Caldwell

The Parkhouse

Edward H. Dewey built this elaborate residence in 1898, which overlooked Lake Ethel in Lakeview Park. Lake Ethel was a man-made irrigation reservoir that filled the lower part of Lakeview Park until it was drained in the mid-1920s. Dewey became Nampa mayor in 1909. Edward was Col. William H. Dewey's son. Col. Dewey was a miner from Silver City and major developer in Nampa.
Photo submitted by Marjorie Williams of Nampa

A Wedding Portrait

George and Clarinda Martineau pose for their wedding photo on Nov. 6, 1906. They were married in St. Paul's Church. George came to Nampa from Montreal, Canada in the early 1900s. He traveled to Nampa with some of Clarinda's family. They settled in the Deer Flat area. Clarinda came with the rest of her family later, and she and George were married soon afterwards.

Photo submitted by Ve Yonne Schell of Nampa

Bale Children

All dressed up, with perky ribbons in the girls' hair and suits for the boys, the Bale children are pictured in 1907. The Bale family came to Canyon County on the train from Michigan.

They settled on a homestead in the Ten Davis area east of Parma. The parents, Roy and Alice Bale, later had five more children. Pictured here are, from left, Bertha, Stanley, Letha, Grace and Bernard Bale.

Photo submitted by Helen Mattox of Nampa

10th Grade Class
Tenth graders at Lakeview High School pose on the front steps of the school during the 1899-1900 school year.
Photo submitted by Vera Palmer of Nampa

A Cowboy Postcard
Cowboys stage a poker game with guns drawn in this 1908 post card.
Photo submitted by Lola Frost of Weiser

Football Team of 1906
The 1906 College of Idaho football team is photographed in front of the Administration Building in Caldwell.
Photo submitted by Helen Olsen of Wilder

The Old Timers

This is a 1908 photo of some of the earliest pioneers of Caldwell, including Riley Cox, third from the right in the back row. Cox came to Caldwell immediately after the Civil War. He rode the train to Kelton, Utah, and then saved money by walking the rest of the way to Caldwell. He opened Caldwell's first drug store with the money that he saved on the train fare. Also pictured are, top row from left: Charles Robertson, blacksmith, farmer; Thomas Andrews; the Rev. Benjamin Franklin Morrow, Dixie; John Mammen, John B. Smith, Middleton; Thomas Norris, farmer; Matt Cook (uncertain, could be William Gess); Cox; Byron Frost; Lewis F. Cook. In the next rows are: Emma (Curtis) McKenzie Fowler; T.W. Boone (or may be Robert McGuire); Capt. John M. Bowman; Prior Burnette; Dr. Junius B. Wright; Lewis Morrow; Isaac (Tobe) Froman; Ferman L. Keller; Laura McGuire; Mrs. Frank Gilbert; Frank Gilbert; Mrs. Emma Mathews; Andrew Jackson Reagan; Alice McKenzie Frost; William Reagan; Charles F. Madden; Tom Johnston; Mrs. Louisa Fouch Clark; James Epperson; Mrs. Arvilla Shipley Paul; Mary Ward; Michael Reed Jenkins; Mrs. Margaret Jobe Newland; Charles Peterson, first Postmaster west of Middleton.
Photo submitted by Lita Boatman of Caldwell

Serpentine Dancers

Downtown Caldwell was the scene of merriment and dancing after each pep rally at the Albertson College of Idaho. Traditionally, the students would form a serpentine dance line and parade through the streets. These 1926 co-eds are hurrying to join the long line of students ahead. *Photo submitted by Lola Frost of Weiser*

College of Idaho, 1910

This is a picture of Sterry Hall on the campus of the College of Idaho in Caldwell on April 20, 1910. The picture was made into a postcard and sent to Mrs. Charles Campbell of Sweet, Idaho. *Photo submitted by Don Johnson of Caldwell*

Class of 1918

The Class of 1918 at the College of Idaho poses for a photo. Only about four-fifths of the class was there for the photo. *Photo submitted by Justine Gowen Hopper*

Diggs Family Stock
The Homer Diggs family shows off some livestock on Urban Martineau's Nampa farm in 1914. Pictured, from left, are Lottie Diggs, who is pregnant with Gladys; Homer Diggs and Mae Diggs. Pug, the dog, is guarding the group and Pet and Bird are the horse team. *Photo submitted by Gladys Messer of Nampa*

Roswell Parma Picnic
The horses and carriages wait patiently while their owners enjoy the festivities and field games at the 1912 Roswell-Parma picnic along the Boise River. This gala picnic began in 1905 at the Frank Howard farm in Roswell for former residents of Minnesota and Illinois. Others were welcome, and so many people began attending each year that the event was moved to the big grove on the H.C. Anderson farm, two miles north of Parma. Crowds eventually exceeded 5,000 and the whole lower Boise community had to pitch in and help. *Photo submitted by Don Johnson of Caldwell*

Happy Valley School
The students of the first Happy Valley School line up to have their picture taken in 1911. Landscaping was obviously not a major concern in early days. A brick school house was built to replace this wooden one a few years later. *Photo submitted by Velma Sanders of Nampa*

Arbor Day, 1915

Gov. Moses Alexander, in the center with a shovel, helps plant a tree at the new grade school in Melba to celebrate Arbor Day in 1915. A bottle with 10 of the children's names in it is buried at the base of this tree. *Photo submitted by Madge Wylie of Melba*

Ten Davis School

The students of Ten Davis School pose for a picture in 1911. The two-story school, no longer in existence, was located between Parma and Notus on Gotch Road. It had four rooms, with two grades in each room, from first through eighth grade. The covered wagons on each side of the building served as school buses. Letha Bale, Grace Bale and Stanley Bale attended this school.
Photo submitted by Helen Mattox of Nampa

Learning to Sew

The Happy Valley School's sewing class works industriously as the teachers look on in this 1915 photograph.
Photo submitted by Velma Sanders of Nampa

Nap Time
A guy can get pretty tired hunting. Ben and Louis Anketell catch 40 winks in their camp back in 1912.
Photo submitted by Marjorie Williams of Nampa

Furry New Stoles
Emma and Harriet Anketell show off their new fur stoles in 1918. The sisters were valedictorians for their respective classes of 1913 and 1914 at Kenwood High School in Nampa.
Photo submitted by Marjorie Williams of Nampa

The Rowland Rig

J. Fred Rowland displays his handsome rig and horses in 1910 in downtown Caldwell. He later became the chief of police in Caldwell.
Photo submitted by Lita Boatman of Caldwell

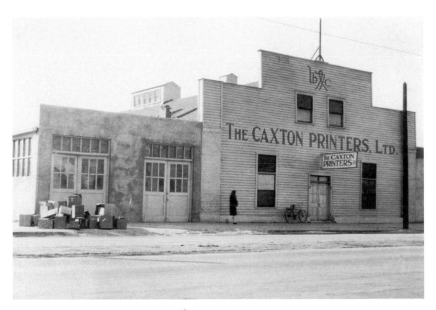

Caxton Printers, Ltd.

This is the original look of the Caxton Printers building in Caldwell around 1915. Later renovations expanded the business. Caxton Press is one of the oldest publishing businesses in the West.
Photo submitted by Jean Wilkerson of Nampa

Taking a Break

Herman Hostetler takes a break from delivering groceries in Nampa, sometime between 1913 and 1917. Oh, for the days of three-digit phone numbers, like the one on his truck's door.
Photo submitted by Vertie Hostetler Bailey of Nampa

Caldwell's Oldest Social Club

Members of the U.T.C., Caldwell's oldest social club, pose for a picture in 1921 or 1922 at the Stiles Ranch in Caldwell. The club, whose name is a secret, was founded in March 1902 by Orinda Stiles, Lina Gipson and Phoebe Jones, for "pure and simple relaxation." Charter members also included Eliza Miner, Flora Miller, Nannie Greenlund, Mary Phillips, Isabel Dee, Ordella Horn, Sadie Johnson, Celia Cowden, Elizabeth Wyngarden, Barbara MacKensie, Gertrude Maxie and Mary Marlott. Membership is limited to 20, by invitation only.
Photo submitted by Ruth Robertson of Greenleaf, the great-granddaughter of Orinda Stiles

Girls Basketball

The 1912 Caldwell girls basketball team. The uniforms worn by the team members reflect the modest viewpoint of society in regards to women in sports during the era.
Photo submitted by Justine Gowen Hopper of Caldwell

Going Camping
The Rose family loads up the wagon to go camping in 1916. Even though the Roses lived in the rural, untamed area of Deerflat, they still liked to get away from it all.
Photo submitted by Leota and Gilbert Rose of Boise

What's This?
Even a piece of straw can be fascinating to a child. Harold Backer inspects his straw find in 1919, while his dad, Dan Backer, takes a break from plowing on their Lone Tree farm.
Photo submitted by Betty Brandau of Melba

The Water Wagon
In dry Idaho country the water wagon was an important part of a farm family's life in 1916. It held the water for all the family's needs. When ice was available they would pack the top of the wagon with it to try to keep the water cool. Shown are Estelline, Ima, Guy, William, Franklin, Charley and Thomas Rose.
Photo submitted by Leota and Gilbert Rose of Boise

Leveling the Homestead
Thomas G. Rose, left, and Franklin L. Rose are leveling the ground on their homestead in 1916 in the Deerflat area, after the land had been cleared of sagebrush.
Photo submitted by Leota and Gilbert Rose of Boise

Nampa Blacksmith Shop

Workers and customers pose for this picture of the blacksmith shop between 1910 and 1912 in Nampa. This is the current site of the Nampa Fire Station. Dr. Frank Hostetler, Nampa's first veterinarian, is the second person from the left. *Photo submitted by Vertie Hostetler Bailey of Nampa*

A Homemade Wagon

Lois Eichenberger pushes her little brother Wilbert on their homemade wagon around 1918. The children loved to play on the hills near their home on Randolph Road, north of Melba. Their parents, Carl and Bertha Eichenberger settled their homestead in the early 1900s. Carl was a founder of the Melba Feed and Seed and Lumber Company in Melba.
Photo submitted by Pat VanOrder of Nampa

The Redmond Home

S.S. Redmond, his wife, Mary, and his son, Lee, pose for a picture in front of their home in 1902. The family moved from Madison, Kan., in 1900. They farmed about 40 acres northeast of Nampa, and Lee walked through the fields to attend Lone Tree School.
Photo submitted by Vera Palmer of Nampa.

Bumper Crop
Blaine Lee, "Uncle" Bud Spillman and Dale Lee
show off 1919's bumper crop of pumpkins.
Photo submitted by Lester and Ruth Allen of Nampa

Footlong Potatoes
Frederick Hoadley displays the best of his 1918 crop of potatoes,
which measured a foot long. He homesteaded 80 acres southwest
of Caldwell on Karcher Road in 1908. He was married with four
children before coming to Idaho from Kansas.
Photo submitted by Shirley Oehler of Caldwell

Working on the Bench

Circa 1910. A crew worked to build the flume on the Roswell bench and extend the irrigation water to that area. These photos show the progression of the building of the flume, culminating in the successful irrigation of the Bench. The last photo (above) shows a happy Walter Obendorf standing on a newly irrigated field.

Photos submitted by Irma Cox of Caldwell

Going to the Festival

All dressed up, the Backer family has its picture taken before heading for the Harvest Festival Parade in Nampa in 1918. Little Bill Backer mimics his father Chris's pose as they sit on the running board of their car.
Photo submitted by Betty Brandau of Melba

A New Motorbike

Frank Lynch gets ready to take his sweetheart, Pearl Mussell, for a ride on his new Indian motorbike in 1912. He was very proud of his new bike. Lynch was the station agent at the Caldwell Railroad Depot. Mussell worked for the telephone company.
Photo submitted by Helen Olsen of Wilder

Parma Railroad Station

Frank Lynch, second from left, poses with the crew at the Parma Railroad Station in 1914. Lynch was the station agent and he and his family moved where the railroad sent them. He was also in Caldwell and later moved to Baker City.
Photo submitted by Helen Olsen of Wilder

Pretty New Hats

Oh, for the hats of yesteryear! Charlotte Berg and Lillian Mussell proudly show off their new hats around 1910. The hats were purchased from Madam Gilgan Sarchets' hat shop in Caldwell, and the young women went to Lillian's sister Myrtle's studio in downtown Caldwell to have their picture taken.
Photo submitted by Helen Olsen of Wilder

A Bumper Crop of Barley

C.C. Hendrickson shows off his barley crop in the 1920s. He farmed 40 acres southeast of Nampa and the farmland remains in the family today. The land was covered by sagebrush when Hendrickson settled on the property in the Southside Boulevard District. Hendrickson traveled from Iowa to Texas to California before coming up the West Coast and moving into Idaho. He worked for John Hodge as a farm hand and then married Hodge's daughter, Myrtle, and settled next to Hodge's farm. *Photo submitted by Esther Harrison of Nampa*

After the Fire

This picture was taken of down-town Nampa, from the water tower after the fire of 1909.
Photo courtesy of the Canyon County Historical Society

A Temporary Home

This is the temporary storefront, set up in 1909, after the Elver & Co. Clothing Store was damaged in the fire. James Strode and Vic Elver were partners in the downtown Nampa store, and specialized in men's clothing, hats and shoes.
Photo submitted by Dottie Neher of Caldwell

Caldwell High Track, 1912
The Caldwell High School Track Team
of 1912 poses for a picture.
Photo submitted by Clarke "Crusty" Hamon of Nampa

Caldwell Basketball
The 1911 Caldwell High School basketball team.
Photo submitted by Shirley Simpson of Nampa

Nampa Skyline, 1914
Lloyd Lumber Co. is a prominent feature on the Nampa skyline, looking north from the water tower in 1914.
Photo submitted by Marjorie Williams of Nampa

Nampa's Main Street, 1920
Main Street in downtown Nampa is depicted in this 1920s photo. Calkins Hardware is located in the bottom left of the picture.
Photo submitted by Dan Braudrick of Nampa

Flood of 1910

Flood waters invaded downtown Caldwell in 1910. This view is taken from the corner of 7th and Arthur facing the "new" City Hall.
Photo submitted by Lita Boatman of Caldwell

Caldwell Train Wreck

Spectators gather around this train wreck outside of Caldwell in the early 1900s. *Photo submitted by Grace Iverson of Caldwell*

Mason Creek Flooding

A milk truck on its way to the creamery crosses the Mason Creek bridge during the flood of 1916.
Photo submitted by Thelma Henson and Ann Henry of Nampa

The Huree Theatre
Caldwell residents take a buggy ride to the old Huree Theatre in 1917. Horace Crookham was the film operator. He later died in a fire.
Photo submitted by Alice Witzig-Smith of Caldwell

Break Time at Adams Cigar Store
Bill Leslie of Calkins and Leslie Cement Contractors, and Enis Campbell of Troy Laundry enjoy a break at the Adams Cigar Store with owner Ed Adams in 1910. The store was located at 110 S. 7th St., Caldwell.
Photo submitted by Alice Witzig-Smith of Caldwell

The Professor's Staff

Professor Cumming, center, with staff of the Middleton School in 1916. From left, Murnie Hadsall, Miss Earnest, Tressie Nickerson, Prof. Cummings, Myrtle Mussell, Eunice Jones and Miss Hammer. *Submitted by Helen Olsen of Wilder*

Middleton High

Middleton High School around the turn of the century. *Submitted by Helen Olsen of Wilder*

Roosevelt School in the Country

Students attending Roosevelt School in the Nampa area pose for their Class of 1912 photo. Teachers were Miss Dryden and Miss Proech. *Photo submitted by Thelma Henson and Ann Henry of Nampa*

Caldwell Baseball Team

Members of the 1908 Caldwell Ladies Baseball Team take a break to pose for a team photo. *Photo submitted by Alice Witzig-Smith of Caldwell*

The Caldwell Methodist Church

The Methodist Church at 123 S. Kimball, stands tall above the unpaved streets of Caldwell in 1890. It was a model of neatness and had an outstanding chapel organ. But the noise from the livery stables and blacksmith's shop, plus the Sisson Hotel, was disruptive, so the church decided to move down Kimball to a larger lot. When the mover got the church astride Indian Creek's wooden bridge at South Kimball and Blaine streets in the middle of a snowstorm, he decided the job was too complicated and, as the story goes, "took off." Finally the church made it to its new home at 307 S. Kimball.
Photo submitted by Irma Cox of Caldwell

Shipping Out

Clarence Rudge and Leonard Kennedy stand together on the train before leaving for Grey's Harbor, Wash. The two were members of the militia before being shipped out to serve in the military circa 1912.
Photo submitted by Grace Iverson of Caldwell

Thrashing Wheat
Farm workers thrash wheat in Canyon County in 1912. *Photo submitted by Grace Iverson of Caldwell*

Last Day at Sunny Ridge

Teachers, parents, kids and younger siblings are captured in this photo on the last day of the school year in 1918 at Sunny Ridge School in Nampa. The third person from the far right is Addie Blakeslee, who named the school Sunny Ridge.
Photo submitted by Lester and Ruth Allen of Nampa

Mrs. Bixby's Sunday School Class

The Middleton Sunday school class of Mrs. G. Bixby poses for a picture around 1910. Luella Manning (Mower), second from left in the bottom row, received a copy of the photo as a gift from her teacher. *Photo submitted by Edward Mower of Nampa*

Middleton Elementary, 1910

Note the high-button shoes and the boys in caps as they pose for a student body photo at the old Middleton Elementary School around the year 1910. The school included grades 1 to 8. It burned down and was replaced by the present Middleton School.
Photo submitted by Edward Mower of Nampa

NNC Campus

The Northwest Nazarene University (formerly College) campus stands alone in this photo from the 1920s. The building in the left of the picture is the University's current administration building.
Photo submitted by Margaret Koolhof of Nampa

Lake Lowell Cool Down

A group of Nazarene Sunday School girls cool off at Lake Lowell in spring 1925. After the class, one of the girls, Josie Hall, chased the others with lizards she had caught. They enjoyed a wiener roast before setting out for home. Teacher Mrs. Ednie made sure they made it home before dark. Included in the photo are Grace Adams, Ruth Kennedy, Ruth Wiley, Josie Hall, Hazel Williams, Ethel Raff and Phylia Raff. *Photo submitted by Margaret Koolhof of Nampa*

Ancient History Class

The Northwest Nazarene College Ancient History class of 1924/25 squints into the sun in this 1925 photo. Lawrence Parsons is in the first row, far left. Margaret Parsons, in the second row, far left, attended all sixteen years of school on the NNC campus. She began the first grade at the elementary and graduated from the college in 1931. *Photo submitted by Margaret Koolhof of Nampa*

Dancing on Lake Lowell
People crowd into a dance pavilion that operated by Lake Lowell in the 1920s. The trolley took people to the lake to spend summer evenings listening to bands and dancing by the water. *Photo submitted by Alice Witzig-Smith of Caldwell*

Potatoes on Dry Lake
The Miller Family in 1920 in the field together during the potato harvest on their Dry Lake farm.
Submitted by Dorothy Miller of Nampa

A Dry Lake Farm
This 1920 Dry Lake area family had to haul water in buckets in order to keep their melon plants alive.
Submitted by Dorothy Miller of Nampa

Caldwell's Saratoga Hotel

The Saratoga Hotel, located at the corner of Main and 7th in Caldwell, was remodeled in 1923, when the top floor was added. Cost of the project was $65,000. The hotel was built in 1904 for a reported $40,000. In one of its rooms, Harry Orchard plotted the assassination of Gov. Frank Steunenberg. *Photo submitted by Alice Witzig-Smith of Caldwell*

The Father of Music

J.J. Smith, far left, was known in Caldwell as the "Father of Music". Smith was the first director of instrumental music at the College of Idaho. All of the Smith's boys went to work for Walt Disney's music department. The oldest son Paul, not pictured, won an Academy Award for Pinocchio. Pictured from left, J.J. Smith, Anna Smith, sons George and Arthur. *Photo submitted by Arlynn Anderson of Caldwell*

Notus Football

Lynn Spillman, in suit, coached the Notus football team to only one loss during the 1929 season. Pictured from left, C. Davis, W. Francis, K. Langdon, W.J. Evans, B. Boatman, W. Pease, W. Kellogg, W. Hodgeson, L. Holmes (Captain), E. Dietrich and C. Roberts.
Submitted by Arlynn Anderson of Caldwell

Notus School

Notus School circa late 1920s. At the time, the school housed all 12 grades. Now it is home to the town's grade-schoolers.
Photo submitted by Arlynn Anderson of Caldwell

Downtown Caldwell, 1920
Caldwell's City Hall and trolley are shown in the background of this 1920s photo. The city building, built in 1907, also housed the fire department, police department, jail and library. The building was later torn down.
Photo submitted by Alice Witzig-Smith of Caldwell

A Rhodes Family Portrait
The Rhodes family of Nampa is pictured in 1915. Sidney and Annie Rhodes came from Ray County, Mo., in 1901. They had a total of 11 children, including Roy, Paul, Joe, Fred, Ottie and Ruth, all born in Missouri; and Dick, Kay, Laura, Lois and Helen, born in Nampa. They arrived in a railroad coach and stayed in a boarding house for a while. Then they had 5 acres and a small house along Mason Creek, between 11th Avenue and 6th Street North. Later they homesteaded on 160 acres northeast of Nampa between what are now Birch and Cherry lanes. The Dewey Palace was being built, and the eldest child, Ottie Rhodes DeCoursey, said her father took her and her brother Roy to see the Grand Opening. Ottie also saw the big hotel torn down.
Photo submitted by Barbara Rhodes of Nampa

Rosenlof Service Station

Edgar Rosenlof shows off the family's service station in 1928. It was built by Edgar's father, Frank, in the late teens and, at the time the photo was taken, it was one of only three service stations in the area. Edgar took over station operations when his father retired.
Photo submitted by Thelma Henson and Ann Henry of Nampa

Nampa Tourist Park

In an effort to boost the area economy, the Nampa Tourist Park was built in the 1920s to draw tourists that might otherwise drive past Nampa.
Submitted by Thelma Henson and Ann Henry of Nampa

Canyon County Courthouse

The Canyon County Courthouse in Caldwell is pictured in the 1920s.
Photo submitted by Alice Witzig-Smith of Caldwell

Caldwell Sanitarium

The Caldwell Sanitarium is shown in this photo from the 1920s. The private hospital declared that it was "prepared to give up-to-date service in surgical, medical and obstetrical cases." Staff included Martha A. Higgs, surgical nurse; F.M. Cole, surgery and general medicine; C.M. Kaley, eye, ear, nose and throat and general practice; S. B. Dudley, obstetrics and general medicine; Ida Kullander, superintendent; and Love Miller-Smith, secretary-treasurer. *Photo submitted by Alice Witzig-Smith of Caldwell*

Caldwell Public Library

The Caldwell Library is photographed in the 1920s. It was built in 1914 with an appropriation of $12,500 from the Carnegie Corporation. *Photo submitted by Alice Witzig-Smith of Caldwell*

Amos Miller Ranch

Amos Miller took a train to Caldwell, Idaho, in 1908, where a real estate dealer named Ross Madden drove him west of Greenleaf and showed him a quarter section of land. All it needed was water and that was on the way. Amos bought the section of land and returned to Wisconsin. His wife Virgie was pleased and the family loaded up and took the train to Caldwell. Amos' son Fred and a neighbor built the house and the family moved into it the fall of 1908. Water had to be hauled from the Roswell Ditch until a well was drilled. In this photograph, Amos, Virgie and Helen are in the buggy while the other daughters are seen here and there. *Photo submitted by Clarke "Crusty" Hamon of Nampa*

Turkey Derby

Glenn Koch races his turkey "Spotless" in downtown Caldwell's annual Turkey Derby in 1948. Caldwell merchants sponsored the race annually on the Saturday before Thanksgiving. The turkeys would be raced down Main Street for one block. Afterwards, customers would compete in contests to win the turkeys for their Thanksgiving dinner. Koch won the derby in 1948.
Photo submitted by Glenn Koch of Caldwell

4th of July Maypole Celebration

Children gather for a Maypole celebration in a Caldwell park during the city's 4th of July celebration in the 1920s.
Photo submitted by Alice Witzig-Smith of Caldwell

Extra, Extra! Get your news here!

Eva May Ogle, right side of photo, tends to The Union News Company newsstand at the Nampa train depot in 1925. Eva was the manager, selling newspapers, magazines, candy and other assorted necessities to travelers on the Union Pacific Railroad. She was transferred to the Boise Depot in 1927. Eva is the mother of Mable Mott (Nissen), the original owner of Mott's Flower Shop.
Photo submitted by Shirley Phillips of Nampa

Fresh Peanuts!

This popcorn wagon was a downtown Caldwell fixture for more than 20 years, starting in 1920. In the late '40s the cart was moved to Arthur Street, about a block from the American Theater.
Photo submitted by Alice Witzig-Smith of Caldwell

Maypole Winding

Students dance and celebrate at the 1924 Maypole winding at Lakeview School in Nampa. Usually held on or around May Day, the Maypole fete was a special event at all the schools.
Photo submitted by Vertie Hostetler Bailey, Nampa, a teacher at Lakeview School

In the Kiddie Parade

"Nampa Boosters" says the sign on their carriage as Earl and Velma Simmons get ready for the Nampa Kiddie Parade around 1925. They are in front of their home at 216 Diamond St., Nampa.
Photo submitted by Orveta Krajnik of Nampa

Swedish Singing Group

Dressed in their colorful native garb, the Swedish Singing Group is captured for posterity. The picture, taken in the late 1920s, features, from the left, Sonja Krave, Reinhold Krave, Mrs. John Burkholtz, four Nazarene students and John Burkholtz.
Photo submitted by Elsa Phelps of Caldwell

On the Merry-go-Round
One of the big attractions at the old Harvest Festival in Nampa was the merry-go-round. The festival was the forerunner of the Snake River Stampede and took place on 12th Avenue South near the present day site of First Security Bank. The picture was taken about 1925 and Orveta Krajnik remembers that the rides were 5 cents when she was a little girl.
Photo submitted by Orveta Krajnik of Nampa

Dressed up for the Nampa Harvest Festival
LaVerda Read Young, left, and Lucinda Arabella Titsworth Young are dressed up for the Nampa Harvest Festival flower judging event where "Grandma Lucy" won first prize for her irises in 1929.
Photo submitted by J.O. Young of Nampa

Fair Produce
A produce display at the Canyon County Fair in the 1920s advertises land for $10 and up.
Photo submitted by Alice Witzig-Smith of Caldwell

Everyone Loves a Parade
A crowd gathers to watch the last of the parade go by on a rainy day in Caldwell in the 1920's.
Photo submitted by Alice Witzig-Smith of Caldwell

Marching Fruit
Children, dressed as fruit, parade down Main Street in Caldwell in the 1920s. *Photo submitted by Alice Witzig-Smith of Caldwell*

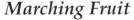

The Men of PFE

The men at the PFE Shop in Nampa pose for a picture around 1935. Huge blocks of ice used to be loaded into the hatches in the top of these railroad cars. The ice blocks weighed about 205 pounds each. At the PFE shop they tore down the box cars and replaced the wood with new wood. For a while they sold the wood to the public at discount prices. When refrigeration replaced the ice blocks, most of the workers were sent to school to learn how to care for the new units.

Photo submitted by Dr. Charles Hanson of Nampa

Soper's Auto Wrecking

Orville Soper stands proudly in front of his business vehicle in 1929. His first shop was at 407 2nd St. S. in Nampa. He built a new shop on the corner of 3rd Street North in 1937. He later served as a mechanic at the Mountain Home Air Force Base during World War II.

Photo submitted by Edward Mower of Nampa

Harvesting the Wheat
Paul Obendorf harvests wheat on his 40-acre homestead on the Roswell Bench around 1920. The wheat was chopped and taken by wagon to the thrashers to separate the grain.
Photo submitted by Irma Cox of Caldwell

A Horsedrawn Combine
The driver looks mighty happy as he rides on the first horsedrawn combine west of Melba in Canyon County in 1929. It is pulled by eight horses and requires three people to operate it.
Photo submitted by Luana Capps of Melba

Idaho's Best Potatoes

Super spuds are Idaho's legacy. In this 1928 photo, Bobbie Reineke, left, and Elizabeth Lovely show off the Reineke farm's "cream of the crop." Farming was a strenuous job in those days. The Reinekes had to haul water from 4 miles away and the nearest neighbor was 10 miles away. *Photo submitted by Luana Capps of Melba*

The Milkman

Jim Longwill poses in 1939 for his first real paying job.
He was paid $90 per month to deliver milk to
homes in Canyon County.
Photo submitted by Darlyne Alekcech of Marsing

Terry's Plumbing and Appliance

Terry's plumbing and appliance store was located in Caldwell
in this undated photo. There were originally two Terry's
plumbing and appliance stores, one in Nampa and one in
Caldwell. TC Blacker purchased the Caldwell store in the 40s
and changed the name to Blackers. In 1954, the Blackers also
began selling furniture. Now the business is Ashley Furniture,
owned by TC's son, Jim Blacker.
Photo submitted by Alice Witzig-Smith of Caldwell

Football Champions
The 1920 Caldwell championship football
team poses for a photo in Caldwell.
Photo submitted by Justine Gowen Hopper of Caldwell

The Women of Basketball
Ready to play, in their spiffy uniforms, are the young women of the
1928 Caldwell Girls Basketball Team. Included in the picture are
Evelyn Tumwan, forward; Edith Shuee, center, Dorothy Beall, guard,
Jessie Lattune, side-center, Bernece Callsen, guard, Emma Howard,
forward, Helen Ramsey, forward Beatrice Amesbury, coach.
Photo submitted by Jean Wilkerson of Nampa

The Students of Cozy Basin School
The bright Idaho sun brings out some squints as the students of Cozy Basin School pose for a school photo in 1929. Cozy Basin School, between Highway 45 and Marsing, was a one-room school with no indoor plumbing. Miss Crockett was the teacher. A big stove provided heat and warmed lunches. Wendell Chase was hired by the school board to be the janitor when he was 11. He was paid $5 a month. He carried water from the well in buckets for the kids to drink. In the back row: Velma McIntyre, Dorothy Cox, Nelma Chase, Joy McIntyre. Middle row: second from left, Ross McIntyre, Jimmy La Vell, Wendell Chase. Front row: on left, Ruth Cox; fifth over, Billy Young; seventh, Lyle Chase.
Photo submitted by Wendell Chase of Nampa

Hayride
In their hats and suits, these ladies and gentlemen look very formal, but in fact they are all on a hayride in Canyon County, around the 1920s. Usually the wagon would travel to Lake Lowell where a picnic would be held.
Photo submitted by Orveta Krajnik of Nampa

Kenwood School
In 1910 the Kenwood School in downtown Nampa is an impressive building. It was located where Home Federal now stands, at 500 12th Avenue South.
Photo submitted by Dan Braudrick of Nampa

A Kenwood School Class Photo
Students from Nampa's Kenwood School pose for a class photo in 1921. Chet Eaton is the first person in the second row from the top.
Photo submitted by Chet and Catherine Eaton of Caldwell

Caldwell's Lincoln School

Lincoln School is an imposing building in this 1920s picture. It housed students from first through seventh grade and stood on the corner of 6th and Cleveland, where the old Sears building now stands. Dorothy Villines remembers B.M. Leach, Mr. Tucker and Mrs. Strain as some of her favorite teachers.
Photo submitted by Dorothy Villines of Caldwell

Going to School

The Chase children snuggle down for the ride to Cozy Basin School, about three miles from their home on the Bowles Ranch near the Snake River around 1924. Pictured are, from left, June, Wendell, Nelma, Fern and Max Chase. The children rode in the pony cart during the winter to keep from freezing.
Photo submitted by Wendell Chase of Nampa

The First School Bus

Lloyd Meyer and Juanita Meyer pose by the first Caldwell school bus in 1924. The picture commemorates the vehicle's first run, before he began transporting the children.
Photo submitted by Dorothy Villines of Caldwell

Van Buren School

This photo of Van Buren School, 1109 Denver, Caldwell, shows the elementary school in the 1920s. Children from first through fifth grade attended at this site.
Photo submitted by Alice Witzig-Smith of Caldwell

A Prize Horse
Albert Lee shows off his prize horse, Babe, in the 1920s in Nampa.
Lee was a county commissioner for 20 years, from 1922 to 1942.
Photo submitted by Lester and Ruth Allen of Nampa

Huston's First Post Office
Anna March proudly stands in front of the first U.S. Post Office in
Huston. Her husband, M.L. March, ran the Post Office and his car
repair shop in Huston from 1920 to 1925.
Photo submitted by John March of Nampa

Family Outing
The Krave family and some friends beat the heat with a frolic at Lake Lowell in the late 1920s. Pictured are Henry, Calla Krave, Vanja Krave, Reinhold Krave, Ivan and their friends.
Photo submitted by Elsa Phelps of Caldwell

Sunny Ridge class photo, 1925
This cheerful looking group is the 1925 class at Sunny Ridge School in Nampa. Kenneth (Dick) Hanson, first row, fifth from left, ran to his house across the street to get his pet rabbit for the occasion. Willard Shroll is in the first row, second from left; Dale Lee is in the second row, first on the left; Charles Hanson is fourth from the left; and Ruth Lee is fifth.
Photo submitted by Dr. Charles Hanson of Nampa

Roosevelt's Fourth Grade Class

Roosevelt School is the new kid on the block — only 6 months old when this picture was taken of the fourth graders in the 1923-'24 school year. Ellen Casler is the first child on the left in the third row. She can remember the coal stove and the path to the outhouse. There were 40 kids in one classroom. Some of the children's names were written on the back of the photo. First row Walter McAbee, Glen, Lester Warren, Oscar Shell, Carl Allan, Allen Hart, Allen Hatfield, Allen Grant. Second row: Glen Clark, Alfred Curtis, John Applegate, Edward ?, Chester Eaton, Ivan Pfaff, ? De Vorss, Sheldon Timmon, Ralph Spangy, Clarence Burman. Third row: Ellen Casler, Ruth Sapp, Doris Manning, Valerie Angel, Zelda Van Houten, Doris ?, Jeannie Ednie, Lily Mae Ednie, Helen Terwilliger, Helen Curtis, Margaret Palmer, Geraldine McCain, Julia Jones. Back row: Ruth Sanders, Kathryn Ruthhart, Miss Quinn (the teacher), and Evelyn McGill.
Photo submitted by Ellen Casler of Nampa

New Glendale School's Class

The first students of the new Glendale School in the Melba area assemble in front of the brick building in the 1920 -21 school year. The school had first through eighth grades. The former schoolhouse was made out of timber. *Photo submitted by Luana Capps of Melba*

Sunday Coffee Trip

The Nystrom family enjoys their Sunday coffee trip in the Nampa sagebrush in 1928. Seated are Elsa Nystrom, Ruth Nystrom (Lombardi) and Mrs. Carl Nystrom. Carl Nystrom is the driver. The family would head for the sagebrush every Sunday for coffee cooked on an open fire. Sometimes they would have cake with their coffee as a special treat. *Photo submitted by Elsa Nystrom of Nampa*

A Williamson Snapshot

Henry C. "Hank" Williamson holds the hand of Winifred Copenhaver around 1922 in front of Grandma Lucy Young's home at 1624 2nd St. N., Nampa. Williamson was an early employee of Morrison-Knudsen. He was also a World War I veteran who had been gassed in combat and suffered effects from that all his life. In the early 1930s, Williamson went into fox farming in the Meadows Valley. He later moved to Sunny Slope where he purchased the orchard owned by his brother-in-law, Ed Gammon. In 1947, Gammon entered the office on the fruit farm and shot Williamson to death. He then went down the ditch bank and shot and killed himself. The present owner of the orchard is Williamson's nephew, Jack Williamson.
Photo submitted by J.O. Young of Nampa

3rd Grade at Roosevelt School
Students attending third grade at Nampa's Roosevelt School pose for this class photo with teacher Miss Patterson in 1922.
Photo submitted by Sandra Humiston of Melba

Roasting Time
Looking rather spiffy in hats and coats, the Lakeview School teachers get their sticks ready for a wiener roast. The picture was taken during 1923 or '24. Some of the teachers are not identified. In the top row, at the right, is Alma Crawther; third from right is Lucy Morton, the principal. Vertie Bailey is second from the left in the bottom row; Vera Trumble, third; and Aline Cohen, fifth.
Photo submitted by Vertie Hostetler Bailey of Nampa

A Horse Hello
Grandpa Gibbs introduces granddaughter Eileen to a horse in the
Dixie Flats area near Parma in 1922.
Photo submitted by Eileen Dunlap of Nampa

In the Garden with Ida
Ida Miller tends to her garden on the family farm outside Nampa
during the 1920s. *Submitted by Dorothy Miller*

Hauling Potatoes

Marion Reineke gets ready to haul a load of sacked potatoes at the Reineke farm west of Melba, circa 1920. The potatoes were then hauled by horse and wagon to Nampa, where they were sorted and shipped to Chicago in a refrigerated rail car.
Photo submitted by Luana Capps of Melba

Hay Stacking

Hay stacking has changed a great deal through the years. This is the way it was done, with a Gowen Derrick, in the 1920s on the A.A. Witteman 40-acre farm. The farm, on the corner of Orchard Avenue and South Florida Avenue, is now owned by Earl Tuckness.
Photo submitted by John and Roberta Witteman of Nampa

A Water Truck

A 1920s water truck motors along the streets of downtown Caldwell.
Photo submitted by Alice Witzig-Smith of Caldwell

Tin Lizzy
Eunice Henley shows off her old "Tin Lizzy" and its decorations in 1929 in Caldwell. The young people would write all over the old cars and then drive up and down the road, just for fun.
Photo submitted by Eunice Lee of Adrian, Ore.

Hunt's Grocery and Service Station
Harvey Hunt owned Hunt's Grocery and Service Station in Roswell, which also housed the Roswell post office.
Submitted by Eledes McConnel of Seattle, Wash.

In The Office
Earl B. Crooks relaxes after organizing his new office for the May 21, 1921, opening of C-B Oil Co. on First Street South in Nampa.
Photo submitted by Louis Reichart of Nampa

The Ideal Food Store

The Ideal Food Store staff poses for a photo in the late 1920s. Pictured from left to right are Frank Blecha, Jess Bermensolo, Ann Bahrychuk Hlastala, Vince Blecha, Rose Blecha, Henry Blecha and Anna Blecha. The store was located on 3rd Street South in Nampa where the Plum Tree furniture store and restaurant now sits.

Photo submitted by Frank Blecha of Nampa.

Nampa's First Buick Garage

Workers at Nampa's first Buick garage pose for a photo in the summer of 1920. Paul Snyder, center, owned the garage while Orval Tillis, left, was a mechanic. Paul Snyder put together a Ford Model T from parts when he moved to Nampa in 1918. The garage had no floor hoist and all the work was done manually. Also pictured is Ross Snyder, Paul's brother, who later became Superintendent of Mail at the Post Office.

Photo submitted by Eldon and Nellie Snyder of Nampa

The Liberty Bell

An estimated 10,000 people flocked to the Caldwell train station to see the Liberty Bell on July 12, 1915. The bell was en route from Philadelphia to San Francisco, and made only four stops in Idaho: Caldwell, Boise, Pocatello and Weiser. After the bell left the city, a patriotic meeting, parade, and baseball game between Ontario and Caldwell took place. That evening there was a band concert at Lake Lowell and a grand ball.
Photo submitted by Alice Witzig-Smith of Caldwell

On the Peirsol Farm

J.N. Peirsol, bottom left, and son Bryan work to oil up the hay derrick on their farm in 1925. The Peirsol family moved to Nampa from Nebraska in 1913 where they bought 160 acres north of Melba from the state of Idaho. They grew hay, grain and potatoes. They also raised sheep, cattle and hogs. The farm remained in the family until the 1980's.
Photo *submitted by Robert Peirsol of Nampa*

Notus All-Conference
The 1928-1929 Second Team All-Conference Notus girls basketball team only lost three games that season. Back row, from left, M. Vail (Capt.), M. Hanafin (All-Conference), B. Albertson and R. Henry. Front row, from left, A. Jackson, R. Henderson and H. Hodgson.
Photo submitted by Arlynn Anderson of Caldwell

Taking a Dip
Florence Fender enjoys a cool dip in Lake Lowell in 1925. Florence was the leader of the Campfire Girls and would often take the group on campouts at Lake Lowell. The girls would swim all afternoon and evening. When they got up each morning, leaders would make them put on their cold, wet swimming suits and go back down to the lake to wash.
Photo submitted by Eunice Lee of Adrian, OR

Gross Family Reunion

On Sept. 10, 1922, the Gross family poses for a picture during its reunion at Kurtz Park in Nampa. Susanna and Neal Gross came from Tennessee and homesteaded on a 40-acre farm on Happy Valley Road, where they raised their seven children.
Photo submitted by Velma Sanders of Nampa

Little Sister

Eileen Gibbs pushes little sister Eiletta in her baby carriage in the Dixie Flats area near Parma in 1923.
Photo submitted by Eileen Dunlap of Nampa

The First Mercy Hospital in Nampa

Impressive for 1919, this is Nampa's first Mercy Hospital. The groundbreaking was on Dec. 9, 1918, and the hospital opened on Nov. 4, 1919, and began caring for patients Nov. 17, 1919. It had 50 beds and was built with funds from the townspeople, the local Catholic Church and the Sisters of Mercy. It was remodeled, expanded and eventually replaced in 1968.
Photo courtesy of Mercy Medical Center

Graduation Day

Mercy Hospital on 16th and 8th streets in Nampa celebrates Nurses Graduation in 1926. The nuns greet the crowd from the balcony.
Photo courtesy of Mercy Medical Center

Canvas Convent

Due to the limited space at the Nampa General Hospital, located on 11th Ave. South, a remodeled eight room frame residence, dubbed the "Canvas Convent" was the home of the "Sisters" for two and a half years. From left are Sisters Bonaventure Earle, Raphael Rohrer, Alphonsus Mulryan and Sister Stanislaus Peters lived in this tent.
Photo courtesy of Mercy Medical Center

Festival Princess Court

The Harvest Festival Princess Court poses for a picture outside the Dewey Palace Hotel in 1934 in Nampa. The girls, nominated by members of the surrounding communities, enjoyed a formal dinner together at the hotel. Betty Crowther is fourth from the left in the front row.
Submitted by Betty Crowther Young of Nampa

Bug Racers

James Collins sits in a homemade car with Gene Collins and another friend after winning the 1932 "bug race" in Nampa. During the harvest festival, bug races would pit children from Nampa and Caldwell against each other. The homemade cars used Maytag gas engines and were usually made by the boys who drove them.
Photo submitted by Maxine Collins of Boise

Wild Goose Chase
Goose hunters Al Iucker, his sons and friends pose with
their quarry on the Iucker Ranch in 1945.
Photo submitted by Merrilyn King of Nampa

William H. Von Wasmer
William H. Von Wasmer poses for a photo in 1930. Von Wasmer
was the founder of the Caldwell Forwarding Company and
remained active well into his 90s. At age 97, he bought a gas-
powered wheelchair to help him traverse the Caldwell streets.
Photo submitted by Justine Gowen Hopper of Caldwell

Orchard Harvest

Farm workers sort fruit at the Lafe Johnson orchard in the Lakeview area of Nampa in 1937. Included in the photo are Gus Miller, Lois Johnson, Vivian Lathee and Mabel Johnson. Workers would sort fruit in the open air as it was picked. Fruit was then placed on a conveyor belt and a mover filled with water.
Photo submitted by Dorothy Miller of Nampa

A Pulling Contest

Dust begins to fly as William D. Smart watches his cousin Lacey Morgan drive his team of horses in a pulling contest around 1930 in Canyon County. The team weight was 2,400 lbs. and the total load was 4,945 lbs. Smart and Morgan won many contests with this team.
Photo submitted by Lillian Lenz of Caldwell

Harvesting Hay

In the 1930s, the Blecha family harvests hay west of Nampa in the old-fashioned way — with horses. Frank Blecha, center, built the wagon and Henry Kroh, left, and Mike Hlastala help cut the hay with a team of horses and then shock it. The hay was loaded onto the wagon by hand and taken to the stack.
Photo submitted by Frank Blecha of Nampa

A Roadside Chat
President Franklin D. Roosevelt stops to chat with R.H. Young and Herbert Peckham in Wilder in 1939. Roosevelt was on his way to inspect onions in Oregon. *Photo submitted by Mary Young of Nampa*

1930's Potato Harvest
Godfrey Brothers farmed potatoes on small rented
tracts of land totaling over 500 acres in Nampa.
Photo submitted by Sheryl Pedigo-Spinden of Nampa

The Hermit of Snake River Desert
The "Hermit of Snake River Desert," right, poses with his friend
Irvin on his porch at the Cove along the middle Snake River (now
called Halverson Bar) in 1939. "Doc " William E. Hisom was born in
the 1850s in Chicago, Ill., and was of African-American and Native
American parentage. He was a second-generation freeman and a
well-educated graduate veterinarian who moved to Idaho and teamed
up with William White, a miner. In 1900 they settled in Idaho
seeking the fine gold found in the river. After White lost his leg in a
farm accident, around 1913, he left, but Doc Hisom stayed on alone,
gardening, fishing, trapping, placer mining and sewing leather goods
from the hides. He played seven musical instruments and was an
expert photographer. He occasionally shopped for groceries in Melba
and was known by several people there, and enjoyed visitors at his
lonely retreat, four miles up the river from the railroad bridge going
to Murphy. He died on Dec. 26, 1944 in the Nampa hospital and is
buried in the children's section of Kohlerlawn Cemetery in Nampa.
Photo submitted by Madge Wylie of Melba

The Men of Basketball
The 1930 Notus basketball team.
Photo submitted by Gail Gumaer

Roswell Boy Scouts
Boy Scouts from Roswell pose in this photo from 1930 or 1931. Pictured are: Front row: Earl Hinman, Henry Ferrel, Merle Larson, Leroy Mogus, John Yates, Robert Obendorf, James Yates, Glenn Allender, Howard Parsons, Leland Burkett, George Otani. Second Row: Philip Grosvent, Foster Robertson, Harold Allender, Norman Obendorf, Kenneth Berkley, Willard Bennett, Monte Johnson, Eugene Cottier, Hugh Sutton, Wallace Burkett, Sherman Young. Third Row: Ralph Bennett, Dallas Richards, Merle Jenkins, Kenneth Johns, Willard Hunt, Richard Shelton, Junior Shulur, Lester Larson and C. Ben Reavis. *Photo submitted by Frieda Ford of Wilder*

The Roswell Ladies Baseball Team
The famous Glen L. Evans tackle company was the sponsor of the Roswell Ladies Baseball team in 1939. The Vikings team played Notus, Parma and Wilder. Team members included Irma Obendorf, Genevieve Shorb, Orpha Mumford, Pauline Mower, Blanche McCullough and Doris Obendorf.
Photo submitted by Irma Cox of Caldwell

Nampa High School Band of '33

The Nampa High School Band of 1933 practices its marching drills before a football game. The band members' mothers made their hats and capes for the uniform. The band was directed by J.A. (Pop) Winther, the majorette. Pictured are: Row 1, Lloyd Snead, Russell Lundquist, Don McLellan, Ernest Agenbroad, Dale Shroll, Jim Jones, Leland Brown; Row 2, Charles Orutte, Dave Stearns, Karl Kuen, Ruth Babcock, Kenneth Hanson. Row 3, Carl Agenbroad, Bruce McBane, Gertrude Pilant, Oren Mahony; Row 4, Charles Hanson, Michael Henry, Roy Pilcher, Martin Edwards, Elmer Brown, Art Wittinberger and Jim Rudge.
Photo submitted by Dr. Charles Hanson of Nampa

Glee Club

The Nampa High Glee Club in 1935. Irene Wallis, Phylis Hatfield, Faye Mendiguren, K. Boyd Remely-teacher, Alice Hashitani, Liberty Hackney, Thelma Dean, Edith McCain, Edith Woosley, Gladys Jones, Alyce Allen, Darlene Morris, Margaret Brown, Marion Blanksma, Ester Hughes, Grace Rudge, Roberta Slagle, Gaylean Make, June Renstrom, Verla Young. *Submitted by Phylis Hatfield Henry of Nampa*

Henry at the Paint Store

Left to right: Mrs. Fifer, Henry Krave and Mr. Fifer pose for a photo in front of the Forve Paint and Art Store in downtown Nampa during the 1930s. The Fifers owned the store and Henry was an employee.
Photo submitted by Kathy Gannussio of Marsing and Sonja Krave Stephens

The Men of Stone Lumber Company

These serious gentlemen are all employees from Stone Lumber Company, having their picture taken to celebrate the opening of the Pacific Fruit Express shops in Nampa, around 1930. In the first row are Manager John Sites and Lewis Ord. In the second row are Morris LaLande, George Cannell and Roy Simmons, yard foreman.
Photo submitted by Orveta Krajnik of Nampa

Catch of the Day

Three fisher folk head triumphantly home with their catch in the late 1930s. However, the irrigation ditches of Nampa don't seem to be the best source of big fish. They used the screen to catch the fish in ditches off Midway between Karcher and Orchard, and then showed off their tiny trophies just for fun. Pictured are, from left, Omer Thomas, Orveta Simmons and Mr. Barrow.
Photo submitted by Velma Sanders of Nampa

Ring Around the Roses

Laughing children dance in a circle at Miriam Keim's 7th birthday party in Nampa on May 25, 1937. The children include Dorothy Cudd, left, Barbara Ware, Bryce Keim, Don Keim, Robert Keim, Pati Conway and Mary Jean Price.
Photo submitted by Miriam Keim Albright of Nampa

That Good Gasoline

A C-B Oil Co. driver gets ready to make his rounds in the company's truck in 1930 on 1st Street South in Nampa. Earl B. Crooks opened the wholesale and retail company in Nampa in 1921.
Photo submitted by Louis Reichart of Nampa

A Box Wagon

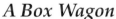

Taking a break from hauling grain, the workers pose for a picture in the box wagon, and light up a cigarette in 1931. The Eaton family used this wagon to haul grain from the thrasher to the granary in Nampa. Pictured are, from left, Leo Rivitt, Jack Morris, Lafe Eaton, Chet Eaton and Mr. Lanbrum.
Photo submitted by Chet and Catherine Eaton of Caldwell

Robert's Meat Market

Frank Roberts tends the counter at Robert's Meat Market in the 700 block in downtown Caldwell in the 1930s. Caldwell's bustling downtown offered everything from food to furniture. Lloyd Meyer was a meat cutter at the market. Many Caldwell citizens will remember going to Robert's as children and getting a free hot dog. *Photo submitted by Dorothy Villines of Caldwell*

A New DeSoto

Wilma, Barbara and Elaine Wilbur stand proudly in front of the family's DeSoto in 1939, just a year after the family had moved from the Kansas dust bowl to Nampa to farm. The family lived on Robison Road and had purchased the car from Showalter Chevrolet in Nampa. The girls became Wilma McCain, Barbara Rhodes and Elaine Rhodes. They were the daughters of Howard and Lottie Wilbur.

Photo submitted by Barbara Rhodes of Nampa.

Second Grade Smiles

The second grade class at Roosevelt Elementary School in Nampa in 1937. Some of the children pictured are: Marion Crowther, Leila Erstein, Gloria Haines, Bill Moore, Barbara Crooks, Edward Laughlin, Benton Long, Harold Antrim, Jimmy Hughes, Roland Hoppins, Ethel Hostetler, Patricia Conway, Billie June Jensen, Mildred John, Jack Baker, Loren Blickenstaff, Kathy Mills, Denise Elder, Winthrop Godfrey, Dale Murphy, Carl Feeler and Gerald Halberg.

Photo submitted by Pati Sweet of Nampa

The Idaho Hillbillies

The Idaho Hillbillies Band members pose for a picture around 1930. Every Wednesday, the band would play on the radio station, KFXD. The group also played for dances around the Nampa area. Pictured in the first row are Elza Harris, Earl McReynolds and Fred Jetter. In the second row are Mr. Riggs, Earl Simmons and Cecil Holmes.

Photo submitted by Velma Sanders of Nampa

May Fete

Charlotte Gibbs looks perky in her "May Fete" costume, around 1935. She is pictured in Lakeview Park in front of a nifty car.

Photo submitted by Eileen Dunlap of Nampa

Harvest Festival Queen of 1936

Dorotha Wall looks lovely in her crown and graceful gown for her 1936 reign as Queen of the Harvest Festival in Nampa.

Photograph submitted by Gerry Rau of Nampa.

A Cool Retreat

These kids enjoy a cool splash in Nampa's swimming pool at Lakeview Park in 1939. Pictured are Robert Fisher, William Fisher and Dick Martin. *Photo submitted by Leota and Gilbert Rose of Boise*

Nampa High Sophomore Football, 1938

The Nampa High School sophomore football team poses for a picture in 1938. Included in the picture are, starting with the top row, Mr. Wagner, V. Beckwith, G. Dentton, L. Simmons, R. Stanley, V. Wood, A. Gardner, R. Kilmer, H. Clark, L. Gilbert, R. Hays, Mr. Brown. In the second row are: R. Watson, B. Towery, J. LaLand, J. Rodwell, W. Howard, R. Johnston, C. Agenbroad, W. Snyder, J. Christenson, R. Moore, W. Garrity. In the bottom row are: E. Vanhouten, F. Murphy, E. Sullivan, F. Blecha, F. Abbott, D. Parks, G. Koyama, W. Stewart, L. Williams, B. Mangum and C. Bridges. *Photo submitted by Frank Blecha of Nampa*

Flying Fish

The men's team of the Malolo "Flying Fish" Swim Team are pictured in 1936 in Caldwell. Present are, bottom row: R.C. Pasley Jr., Jack Robinson, Waldo Stone. In the second row are Pete Kim (instructor), Bill Bozman, Sam Kim, Charles McClure, John Plowhead. In the top row are: Jim Tewell, Luelmer Black, Dean Adams, Ron Streets and Lloyd Tewell. *Photo submitted by Jim Tewell of Caldwell*

Examining the Onions
Part of a Free Press photographic series from the 1930s, this picture shows J.P. Toft and B.E. Kuhns, the county agent, examining the onion crop on the Roy Toft Farm.
Photo submitted by Jane Scroggins of Caldwell

Potato Harvest
This is one of a series of pictures taken of the potato harvest on the Roy Toft Farm by the Free Press photographer. The workers are picking potatoes in the 1930s, a back-breaking job. The boy has the mule tied to his belt.
Photo submitted by Jane Scroggins of Caldwell

The Potato Digger
This Free Press photo shows Howard Toft on the potato digger he invented. He was accompanied by Walt Korte in the 1930s.
Photo submitted by Jane Scroggins of Caldwell

Drill Team Rehearsal

The Southside Grange Drill Team rehearses in Lakeview Park in 1933. Led by Virgilene Tiegs and Ernest Agenbroad, the group practiced twice a week for about two hours each session. The members traveled all around the area to perform for various functions and events. They performed for the National Grange in Boise, the Dairyman's Creamery and in front of the Nampa City Hall.
Photo submitted by Lester and Ruth Allen of Nampa.

A Homemade Airplane

Terrell Chase holds a plane which was made by his brother Max in Melba. The plane had a Bunsen burner inside with a steam engine made out of rifle shells to make it fly. And it did fly!
Photo submitted by Wendell Chase of Nampa

Roosevelt School Minstrel Show

Roosevelt School's fifth and sixth graders gather for a photo at Gowen Field in 1942. The Nampa elementary students put on a minstrel show for the school's student body and for the soldiers at Gowen Field. The master of ceremonies led dancing, singing, marching and comedy skits. The parents made the costumes. Included in the photo are: Beverly Wohlgamuth, Miriam Keim, Jerry Shaver, Billie June Jensen, JoAnn Razon, Warren Russell, Barbara Terry, Bill Moore, Arlen Tidwell, Bobby Wood, Beverly Holms, Shirly Taylor, Majorie McClung, Bryce Keim, Pati Conway, Rose Powers, Bob White, Dee Taylor, Pat Robb, Dolores Momany, Don McKee, Jackie Jarvis, Irma Allen, Norma Wholgamuth, Sally Robb, Sharon Ord, Joyce Allen, Connie Rhodes, Jean Eshelman, Don Machos. *Photo submitted by Miriam Keim Albright of Nampa*

Smile Kitty! Smile for the Camera!
Joy Givens was just a toddler in the late 1930s when she posed for this picture in her wagon, along with her cat who didn't seem to mind the strangle hold. *Photo submitted by Velma Sanders of Nampa*

A Photo with Grandpa
Miriam, Anne and Elizabeth Keim pose for a photo with their grandparents, Emma and Howard Henry Keim, at their Willowdale Farm on Nampa's north side in 1937. Howard Henry Keim was elected mayor of Nampa in 1919. Miriam stands behind her sister Anne, left, and cousin Elizabeth. *Photo submitted by Miriam Keim Albright of Nampa*

Sitting Pretty
Fun-loving Toots Barker poses for an
unconventional photo around 1930.
The setting is the Roy Simmons farm,
where Toots' husband worked.
Photo submitted by Velma Sanders of Nampa

Mr. Conductor
John Patrick Collins stands proudly in
front of the train depot in Nampa in 1936.
He was a conductor and long-time
employee of the railroad.
Photo submitted by Maxine Collins of Boise

Dressed Up and Ready to Go
Here's a young lady all ready to go to the
Maypole competition in Nampa's Lakeview
Park in 1938. Rosie Bahrychuk's lovely
costume included a saucy hat and a parasol.
Each school had its own pole with colored
streamers and a dance to perform to the
music broadcast over the loudspeaker.
Photo submitted by Rosie Millward of Nampa

Drought Relief

Workers layout the pelts collected after sheep were butchered in 1931 in Nampa. The Drought Relief program of 1931 provided sheep so valley residents could butcher them for the meat when food supplies were meager. The pelts had to be returned so the government could track the numbers. *Photo submitted by Marjorie Williams of Nampa*

Alsike Clover Seed Harvest in Lone Tree

Chris Backer and Charlie Shijack have filled their wagons with Alsike Clover seed. The seed was harvested like grain, cut, thrashed and bagged. *Photo submitted by Betty Brandau of Melba*

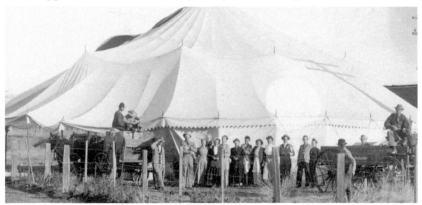

Apple Packing Gang

Apple packers pose for a photo in front of a portable tent that was used at packing time. The photo was turned into a postcard and sent to the mother of one of the packers.
Photo submitted by Don Johnson of Caldwell

Loaded with Onions

This truck, loaded with onions, is parked in front of H.M. Chase Produce in the late 1930s. *Photo submitted by Jane Scroggins of Nampa*

Harvesting Sugar Beets

Times and technology change, but the sugar beets have to get to the factory fast for sweet results. In this 1942 picture, the workers harvest the beets. *Photo submitted by Gladys Messer of Nampa*

Three Men and A Farmall Tractor

Three men harvest the grain in the wheat field south of Nampa with a Farmall tractor on July 23, 1942. Pictured are, from left, Homer Diggs, Floyd, and Archie Diggs.
Photo submitted by Gladys Messer of Nampa

Working at the Hatchery

Workers at Dunlap Hatchery in Caldwell inspect chickens in 1939. Included in the photo is Clyde Mead, Oscar Dunlap, Ralph Dunlap and Gregg Dunlap. *Photo submitted by Faye Dunlap of Caldwell*

The New Dunlap Hatchery

Dunlap Hatchery sits at its "new" location on Cleveland Boulevard in Caldwell in 1946. The Hatchery began in 1918 to breed chickens and eggs and was originally located on 10th Street. In 1929, owners moved the business to Washington Street, then to Cleveland in 1946. *Photo submitted by Faye Dunlap of Caldwell*

Costumed Lassies

These young girls are all decked out in their crepe paper finery to ride on a float in the Nampa Harvest Festival parade in 1932, but one girl seems to have lost her bow. The costumed lassies are, back row, Jonnie Frost, Margret Harrel, Peggie Peterson, Eleanor Peterson and Anna Mae Harrel. In the front row are Geraldine Sandy, Fern Coffman, Bonita Betts and Betty Backer.

Photo submitted by Betty Brandau of Melba

Students of Lone Star School

The first and second grade students of Lone Star School in Nampa are pictured during the 1930 to '31 school year. Their teacher was Miss Gertrude Elliot. In the front row are June Fujikawa, Edward Patterson, Carol McCarty, Frank Hicks, Alice Orr, Oakey Cook. Second row: Imogene Perry, Leroy Blickenstaff, Stella Bennett, Glen Barnhardt, Virginia Cline, Donald Morse. Third row: Claudine Basey, Eldon Snyder, Dorothy Ekstein, George Basey, Helen Chase. Fourth row: Betty Ruegl, Billy Ekstein, Clara Reynolds, Ken, Velma Blickenstaff and Robin.

Photo submitted by Eldon and Nellie Snyder of Nampa

A Skelton Family Portrait

The Skeltons came to the Treasure Valley from Oregon in 1907 and homesteaded four miles southwest of Caldwell on Lonkey Lane. They farmed there for 30 years before retiring and passing the farm to their son Homer. The old farmhouse still looks almost like it did in 1914, and their grandson still occupies part of the homestead. This 1930 photo shows Charles and Louisa Skelton with their children, from left: Walter, Arthur, Homer and Mae. All of the children graduated from Caldwell High School.

Photo submitted by Homer Skelton of Caldwell

Girl Reserves

The members of the Girls Reserves in 1939 pose for this photo. The group focused on learning manners and appropriate social behavior.
From left to right, they are: Row 1: Blossom Simer, Joy Elsar, Florence Sarenberry, Edith Wilson, Grace Bowman, Fay Waltman, Marjory Davis, Mary Evans, Marjorie Anketell, Elaine Hanks, Betty Sutton Row 2: Mamie Stark, Helen Barrett, Glenda Bell, Esther Smalljohn, Arline Stevens, Norma Waltman, Betty Lou Foster, Olive Wilson Row 3: Juanita Oliver, Virgina Sallee, Dorthy Franke, Avis Loaves, Lorraine Nicodemus, Evelyn Hannon, Vila Lawerance, Georgia Noble, Wilma Martin, Nellie Tyler, Clarabelle Nord, Phyllis Miller, June Rosenlof, Frankie Roberts Row 4: Marjorie Johnson, Sonia Good, Maxine Geisler, Dorthea Robinson, Betty Beer, Betty Brown, Thelma Pleumons, Roberta Wogers, Raydean Thompson, Georgia Smythe, Erma Fulcher, Evelyn McNeer, Lorna Lou Buck.
Photo submitted by Marjorie Williams of Nampa

Waiting for the Parade

The children of the Island School outside of Parma gathers for a group photo in 1937. The group is wearing hats in anticipation of a parade in Nampa. Margaret (Parsons) Koolhof taught all eight grades in the school. *Photo submitted by Margaret Koolhof of Nampa*

Roswell Ladies Basketball

Looking very snappy in their monogrammed shorts, the 1936 Roswell Ladies Basketball Team poses with Coach Miss Dilley, right, who wears street clothes and shoes. Team members are, from left, Eledes Hunt, Violet Brown, Freida Riggs, Irma Obendorf, Margaret Allen, Hazel Rock, Doris Obendorf, Arleen Obendorf and Margaret John. *Photo submitted by Irma Cox of Caldwell*

Dance Hall Band

The IOOF dance hall band played the mellow music of the 1945 to '47 era every Friday night in downtown Caldwell for dancers' pleasure. Pictured are Bill Wagner on the drums, Merle Ames on guitar, Weldon Thomas as vocalist, Floyd Ames on bass fiddle, Marvin Henderson on saxophone, Helen Wilber on piano, and Georgia and Verda Ames, sitting at the back.
Photo submitted by Ermal Bowers of Caldwell

Gardiner Homestead

The Gardiner family settled their homestead in 1903 in the Deerflat area. Shown here is the second generation of Gardiners to farm the ground, Lottie and Jocelyn with their daughter Virginia. Lottie and Jocelyn met through an advertisement for "pen pals" in the newspaper. Their daughter, Judy Smith, still lives on a portion of the original homestead.

Photo submitted by Judy Smith of Caldwell

Extra! Extra!

A boy sells a copy of the Idaho Free Press in this 1949 photo taken in front of the Dewey Palace in Nampa.

Photo courtesy of the Canyon County Historical Society

A Bennett School Class

The students from first through fourth grades at Bennett School have their picture taken in 1937. The two-room school was located on the corner of Bennett and Lynwood, and it was torn down in the 1950s. After it closed in 1958 it was combined with Scism School to form a Class "C" District, Scism Elementary SD#138. Some of the children pictured are Doly Martineau, Teresa Budell, Arlie Lyons, Jackie Morris, Junior Martineau, Wayne Blanksma, Joe Ostyn, Elmer Gossett, Marvin Blanksma, Paul Budell and John Witteman.
Photo submitted by Roberta Witteman of Nampa

Rainbow Jane

Jane Toft is proud of her entry in the "Back to School" parade, held at the end of summer 1946 in Caldwell. She won a prize for her costume and decorated bike. Her mother, Bernice, made her rainbow-colored outfit out of crepe paper and her father, Roy, fastened a wire over the bike to hold the rainbow on it.
Photo submitted by Jane Scroggins of Caldwell

Gather at the River

Reverend T. D. Grover baptizes Quentin Douglas in the Boise River outside of Parma in the 1940s. Members of the congregation would always go to the river for Baptisms and would begin the service by singing the old hymn "Shall We Gather at the River."
Photo submitted by Margaret Koolhof of Nampa

East Side First Grade

The first graders at East Side School get their class picture taken in 1933. Before the big East Side School was built, the classes were held in a row of bungalows, with one class per building. Some of the children pictured include, bottom row, left to right, Orveta Simmons (Krajnik), Merle Irish, Frances Campbell, Roy Young, Ralph Wiley, Phyllis Nicodemus, Ilene Wine, Ettie Young, Charles Blanton, and unknown. In the second row are George Rhodes, Phyllis Pepper, T. Carlo, Maxine Brannon, Alberta Bechman, (2 unknowns), Horrace Moffit, Dolores Schmier, Cathleen Bradburn. Third row has Bob Nicodemus and Jack Ziegler. In the top row are teacher Miss Nellie Mathews, Carl Hickey, Patty Still, Bob Pritchett, and Birdie Campbell at the right.
Photo submitted by Orveta Krajnik of Nampa

Delicious Cookies
This picture was taken in 1949 to launch the selling of the famous Girl Scout Cookies.
Front row: Lowana Gould and Sandra Hendry.
Second row: Marilyn Coyle, Mrs. Lola Sadler, and Karlene Warren.
Submitted by Sandra Humiston of Melba

Little Ballerinas
These pretty little ballerinas pose for a quick photo before their annual recital at Central Auditorium in Nampa in 1947. They are, from left, Jeanne Hurt, Vivian Fletcher, Merrilyn Hendry, Mary Courtney and Sharon. They were students of Mrs. Van De Steeg, who taught because she just loved children. She taught boys and girls from 3 to 19 years of age for more than 25 years in her studio in the old Eagle Hall Ballroom at the corner of 11th Avenue North and 1st Street North in Nampa. She said if her students learned "good physical care, grace, poise and the beauty of coordinated movement," then she considered them a success.
Photo submitted by Merrilyn King of Nampa

A Horseback Square Dance

Members of the Huston Mustang Saddle Club practice a square dance on horseback in this photo dating from the 1940s. The group performed at local rodeos and had much fun (and many banged knees). From the left of the dog and around the circle clockwise: Roy and Bernice Toft; Earl and Lola Armstrong; Rosie and Herman Case; Paul and Ethel Hoadley; Chub and Mildred Anderson; and Carl and Mary Platt. Couples in the center of the circle are Virgil and Della Harris on the right and Lowell and Yvonne Prevo on the left. *Photo submitted by Jane Scroggins of Caldwell*

Huston Mustang Saddle Club

Members of the Huston Mustang Saddle Club pose for a group photo in the late 1940s. The group won many blue ribbons at rodeo parades throughout the Boise Valley. The little girl on the pinto pony is Barbara Cooper, mother of champion jockey Gary Stevens. Also pictured as a little girl is Virgina Harris, mother of World Champion Cowboy Dee Pickett.
Photo submitted by Jane Scroggins of Caldwell

Building the Bridge

Tom Carr and his crew pour concrete as they build the bridge across Indian Creek at 7th and Blaine streets in Caldwell in the mid-1930s. The crew had to bring in all the supplies to mix their own concrete on the site. As soon as the mixer was empty, another crew would load more material into the mixer. Carr had the contract to build all 13 bridges over the creek. The Caldwell Depot can be seen at the far end of the street. *Photo submitted by Isobel Carr of Nampa.*

The Farm City Parade

The South Side Grange Float glides through Nampa in the Farm City parade in the late 1940s. The float displayed farm produce in the parade, held every year between irrigating and harvesting. From left: Ila May McClelland, Evelyn Martineau and Inez Gray.
Photo submitted by Lester and Ruth Allen of Nampa

A Puppy Break

James Strode takes a break from work in the 1940s with his dog and a hand-rolled Bull Durham cigarette. James worked for more than 30 years at the Pacific Fruit Express Ice Plant. It was his job to pack ice blocks onto the conveyor belt that led to the "reefers:" refrigerated train cars that held fruit for shipping.
Photo submitted by Dottie Neher of Caldwell

A Mock Wedding

Moose Lodge members put on a mock wedding to entertain fellow members circa 1940. Participants include Ruth Cuff (first in the back row), Velma Thomas (fifth in the back row) and Dorothy Price (the bride).

Photo submitted by Velma Sanders of Nampa

Performing at the Stampede

Eddie Dean and the Rodeo Revelers perform at the Snake River Stampede in 1947. In the background are the Stampede Queen, Rosie Bahrychuk, and her attendants Marcella Gross, Carol Whittenburger, Louise Bloucher, Helen Woodvine and Sally Robb.

Photo submitted by Rosie Millward of Nampa

A Bird's Eye View

August and Grace Noltensmeier came to Idaho from Nebraska in 1937 with daughters Leona and Delores and located on Sunnyridge Road near Nampa. They bought a farm and milk cows and raised chickens, pigs and geese. Neighbors included the McDorams, Ernie Walker, Frank Potter, Vandermeres and Smittys families. They would get together and help each other with harvest. The wives cooked the meals and the work ethic was taught. Son-in-law Stan Graham now farms the Noltensmeier Farm, where Grace still lives.
Photo submitted by Delores Graham of Nampa

Standing in an Ocean of Oats

Porter Lee shows off his oats crop in 1942. Porter was 5 feet, 10 inches tall. A native of Iowa, he moved to Caldwell in 1940.
Photo submitted by Eunice Lee of Adrian, Ore.

Siblings
Eddie and Shirley Chaloupka pose in front of their barn near Parma around 1944. *Photo submitted by Leota and Gilbert Rose of Boise*

Topping Beets
Workers top beets at the Roy Toft Farm in 1945 or 1946. *Photo submitted by Jane Scroggins of Caldwell*

Clearing Sagebrush
Clearing the sagebrush on the farm is a big job. This family would bring food to share and would work together to clear the fields in Middleton in 1949. The women and children shown gathering the brush are, from left, Wayne Stephens, Wilma Reynolds, Pauline Reynolds, Anna Stephens, Noma Reynolds and Kathy Stephens. *Photo submitted by Kathy Gannussio and Sonja Krave Stephens of Marsing.*

Using the Jackson Hay Fork
Omer Thomas is using the Jackson Hay Fork to stack hay in 1940 on the Roy Simmons 120-acre farm, where Midway Road is today. *Photo submitted by Orveta Krajnik of Nampa*

Roosevelt Elementary Basketball

The Roosevelt Elementary School basketball team of 1940 poses in front of the Nampa school. Pictured are: Coach Wesley Steck, Bill Moore, Bob Myers, Dee Taylor, Bob White, Pat Robb, Bob Woods, holding the ball.
Photo submitted by Miriam Keim Albright of Nampa

Nampa Central Girls Basketball

The 1942 Nampa Central Jr. High Girls basketball team. Top row, from left, Lila Ekstein, Dorothy Hergert, Shirley Taylor, unknown. Second row, Pati Sweet and Joyce Allen Beal. Sitting, Dorothy Coates. *Submitted by Pati Sweet of Nampa*

Marilyn's Chicks

This pretty little chick meets some real turkey chicks at the Kratzberg Turkey Farm. Marilyn Sperry, 3 years old, is visiting the 54-acre farm that was owned by Mr. and Mrs. George Kratzberg in 1948. After buying the farm in 1943, the Kratzbergs raised thousands of young turkeys and shipped hundreds of eggs to Iowa and Canada. *Photo submitted by Gail Gumaer of Caldwell*

Stampede Princess

Nampa Stampede Princess Pati Conway sits atop her horse in 1948. At the time, the Stampede Princess was chosen by popular vote by Nampa Free Press readers. S*ubmitted by Pati Sweet of Nampa*

Dean Oliver on Rozy

A 13-year-old Dean Oliver takes Rozy for a ride on the Roy Simmons Farm in 1943. Dean stayed on the farm during the summer to work and Roy took him to rodeos. The future world champion would practice his roping on the farm. *Photo submitted by Orveta Krajnik of Nampa*

70th Reunion

Members of the Horace Luther Straight Class Boise Consistory, 70th reunion, "Ancient and Accepted Scottish Rite of Freemasonry" pose for a photo in 1944. Front row, left to right: J. Robert Matlock, U.S.N.; Homer S. Deal; Wanek Stein; Luster H. Williams; Homer C. Sautter; Edwin G. Wells; Wm. A. Roberts. Second row, left to right: Leo I. Van Luven; Geo. C. Parsons; Capt. John A. Andrews, U.S.A.; Capt. Frederic A. Millerd, U.S.A.; Harold V. Packer, U.S.N.; John Jay Rugg; John D. Snow; Fred W. Nicholson; Dr. Richard D. Simonton; Major Walter E. Burnham, U.S.A.; John F. Rowland. Third row, left to right: W. Penn Stohr; Richard C. Langrell; Cecil J. Curington; Maurice C. Troyer; M. Claire Baldridge; Frank E. Smyth; Walker Dilley; Clarence L. Fiser; Oce. W. Bunton; Russell E. Junior, U.S.A.; Robert H. Ross. Fourth row, left to right: Fletcher B. Johnson; Leroy C. Ehlers; Roy S. White; Wilfred R. Jones; Roscoe Etter; John A. Crowl; Lindon F. Watson; Clarence F. Hanzel; Sidney C. Wade; Guy F. Tarleton. *Photo submitted by Lita Boatman of Caldwell*

Toast Mistresses Club

Charter members of the Toastmistresses Club pose for a group photo in 1952. The organization instructed women how to speak in public. Included in the photo are Ada Christensen and Mabel Mott.
Photo submitted by Shirley Phillips of Nampa

Fairview Market

Fairview Market co-owner August Redinger stands outside his business at 710 Fairview in Nampa in 1953. His wife, Lydia, was a co-owner. *Photo submitted by Janice Walker of Nampa*

Dobbs Brothers

The Dobbs Brothers, Cecil, Everett and Howard, started the Hudson and GMC dealership in 1945. This photo was taken in 1949. It was located at 909 3rd St. S. in Nampa. Later it became a Dodge dealership and was sold to Bob Latham in 1986. Cecil now works with his son Jon who is still in the automotive business in Nampa. *Photo submitted by Jon Dobbs of Nampa*

An Outing with Daddy

Janis McClung Dunn and her dad, Ross McClung, admire the fish pond in Nampa's Lakeview Park in 1943. The park no longer features the pond. *Photo submitted by Janis Dunn of Nampa*

A New Building for KFXD

The new transmitter building for KFXD is photographed in 1968. The radio station's history started in Logan, Utah, in 1925. In March 1927, KFXD aired from Jerome. As the radio industry grew, KFXD was moved from Jerome to Nampa, at 1024 12th Ave. S. By April 1932, auxiliary studios were opened in Caldwell at South 8th and Grant streets, and 11th and Main streets in Boise. A new studio and transmitter building, costing $100,000, was opened Jan. 1, 1938, at the same Nampa site. Today, KFXD is Idaho's third oldest continuously licensed AM broadcast station, and is located at 455 West Amity Road, Nampa, and operates on 580 kHz.

Photo submitted by Dan Braudrick of Nampa.

KFXD'S Doyle Kain

Doyle Kain stands in front of the KFXD radio station in Nampa, where he was a longtime sportscaster and sales representative.

Photo submitted by Leota and Gilbert Rose of Boise

Visiting

Amos J. Miller and Jim Carl, two prominent Caldwell businessmen, turn into horsemen when they visit the old rodeo grounds, *Photo submitted by Clarke "Crusty" Hamon of Nampa*

Fishing at the Wilson Drain Ditch

Glen Reed, along with daughter Glenda and son Donald, enjoys an afternoon of fishing in the Wilson Drain Ditch on their Sunnyridge Road ranch in 1965. *Photo submitted by Lillie Reed, Nampa*

The First Home for Edmark

The first Edmark Dodge-Plymouth building is under construction in this 1927 photo. The building was located at 13th Ave and 2nd St. in Nampa. This is the first of five different locations the dealership would occupy in Nampa.
Photo submitted by Dave Edmark Jr. of Nampa

The Joy of Flight

Dave Edmark Sr. shows off his new Globe Swift airplane at the Nampa airport in 1946. Edmark served in the Navy in World War II, and after returning home he purchased this plane with his brother Bill. Dave enjoyed flying for more than 20 years for business and pleasure all around the United States and Mexico.
Photo submitted by Dave Edmark Jr. of Nampa

Edmark's Second Home

This 1946 photo shows construction of the second Edmark Dodge-Plymouth dealership building at 3rd St and 11th in Nampa. Eventually, Edmark sold that dealership, purchased the Chevrolet franchise and moved to a new building at 345 Nampa-Caldwell Blvd. Now the dealership sells all six lines of GM vehicles as well as Hummer and are expanding to a new location at the Garrity exit of Interstate 84. *Photo submitted by Dave Edmark Jr. of Nampa*

Quitting Time

The entire crew of Idaho Power stands outside the Nampa office at quitting time in 1941. By 1943, Idaho Power was down to a skeleton crew, because so many men had joined World War II. In the background of the photo, the water tower, Dewey Palace and the RV Service shop can be seen. *Photo submitted by Merrilyn King of Nampa*

Working in the Caxton Bindery
The Caxton Printers Bindery Crew poses at the Caldwell printers in 1941 or '42. The crew put together packets of pages to staple or glue. From left: Dorothy Pidgeon, Mary Zink, Ruth Wize, Maxine (last name unavailable) and Euphora Soper Mower. Euphora worked at Caxton's until she got married in 1942.
Photo submitted by Edward Mower of Nampa

Now Open for Business
Orville Cox, left, and Alfred Christensen celebrate the opening of their new auto repair shop in 1946 on 1015 N. 5th Ave., Caldwell. The two bought the shop and became known as "the experts" in car and truck repair. Cox bought Christensen out in 1947 and expanded the business until selling it in 1978.
Photo submitted by Irma Cox of Caldwell

Vermaas Vanways
Jim Vermaas started his Vermaas Vanways business in 1939 during World War II, had 8 employees, and sold it in 1954 to Jerry Mileger. He had a pick-up and delivery service in 1938 that lead him to start Vanways in 1939. *Submitted by Bonnie Vermass of Middleton*

The Crew
The Lindsey Brothers Crew gathers in Nampa in 1949.
Photo submitted by Sheryl Pedigo-Spinden of Nampa

Mercy Nurse Cadets

Looking very snappy in their dress uniforms, this group of nurse cadets from the Mercy School of Nursing in Nampa, pose for their picture in 1944. The students lived in the dorms and attended school for three years from 1944 to 1946. The young women are, from left, Opal Ford, Trini (Goiri) Moad Snow, Laura Caldwell-Messler, Maxine (Micky) Robbins-Maybon, Betty Robbins-Bigler and Marie Arano. *Photo submitted by Micky Maybon of Caldwell.*

Caldwell's First Ambulance

Paramedics stand in front of Caldwell's first ambulance in 1949. In the background is the Caldwell City Hall. *Photo submitted by Alice Witzig-Smith of Caldwell*

Flag Raising

Migrant farmworkers gather at the farm labor camp south of Nampa in 1944 to participate in flag-raising ceremonies, which included the flags of both the U.S. and Mexico. National anthems were also played.
Photo submitted by Verla Harker of Nampa.

Jamboree Royal Court

Nampa children take their place in the PTA Welfare Jamboree royal court in 1946. The children are, from left to right: Dee Macy and Ann Shuck from East Side Elementary, Jimmy Lynch and Ann Rosenlof from Lakeview Elementary, Bruce Everton and Arolyn Adams from Roosevelt Elementary, Mike Robb and Sharon Shea of Kenwood Elementary, and Roy Pearson and Judy LaLande from St. Paul's Catholic School. All children were in the first grade. Proceeds from the annual affair were used to purchase glasses, shoes and medical care for underprivileged Nampa children, as well as film for the school's visual education program.
Photo submitted by Thelma Henson and Ann Henry of Nampa

Entertaining at the Labor Camp
LeRoy Willyerd, center, and two unidentified musicians get ready for a night of entertainment at the farm labor camp south of Nampa in 1944. Willyerd was manager of the camp.
Photo submitted by Verla Harker of Nampa

Cinco De Mayo at the Labor Camp
Two men from the farm labor camp south of Nampa celebrate Cinco de Mayo in 1944 by performing the Mexican Hat Dance. No women were allowed in the camp, so one of the men had to play the role of the female dancer.
Photo submitted by Verla Harker of Nampa

At Chuck's Drive-In
Herman Boston, Lola Boston Remakulus, Thurman Boston, Tina Boston, Mary Boston and Bea Johnson Boston gather next to Chuck's Drive-In in Nampa in the early 1940s. The little boy's name is unknown. *Photo submitted by Carol Boston of Nampa*

Borchert Feed and Coal
The Borchert Feed and Coal truck is all dressed up for the 1949 Nampa Harvest Festival Parade. From left: Jonesy the butcher, Otto Borchert, Alfred Borchert, Arlan Hesse, Walter Choat, Virgil Spitznaugle, Charlie Korn, Walter Borchert. Doug and Sandra Borchert are the children standing on the truck. Otto Borchert and his son Alfred, along with his brother-in-law Don Seitz, bought the store in 1946. Otto's son Walter bought Don out in 1947.
Photo submitted by Echo and Walter Borchert of Nampa

Gym Class

Students from a Central Jr. High gym class in Nampa pose in uniforms worn for their Scottish Sword dance performed in a League of Nations assembly. From left, Joann Snyder, Thelma Plemmons, Bonnie Feeler, Vivian Gott, Joan Hamilton, Lois Baily, Peggy Alverson, Marjorie Yates, Fay Waltman, June Waterhouse, Shirley Schroader, Maxine Geisler, Gloria Welch and Joyce Machos.
Photo submitted by Faye Sturgis of Nampa

Roswell Class Photo

Members of the 1930-31 Roswell 4th and 5th grades pose for a picture. In the fourth grade: Marvin Abbott, Leonard Clary, Ival Freeman, Allen Fretwell, William Goracke, Roy Graham, Clifford T. Mitchell, Oneta Burkett, Virtu Johnson, Jean Steel, Gordon McCormick, Clifford Mitchell, Joe Obendorf, Goerge Otani, Ira Richards, Robert Tuning, Neva Allender, Alta Boyd, Yoshiys Otani, Jewell Keys, Teacher Eleanor McCoy. In the fifth grade: Glen Allender, Fay Burrill, Shirley Callaway, Warren Clary, Merlin Cornwell, Henry Goracke, Walter Obendorf, Bethel English, Irma Obendorf, Thelma Tharrington, Fawn Webb, Helen Wheatley, Robert Obendorf, Donald Robertson.
Photo submitted by Frieda Ford of Wilder

Harvesting the Corn
Allen Noble drives the tractor and Wilmer Harrison is on the combine during the corn harvest of 1948. The Harrisons grew corn, beans and wheat on 80 acres in the Happy Valley School District near Nampa. The Happy Valley School can be seen in the background.
Photo submitted by Esther Harrison of Nampa

The Class of 1931

The 1931 graduating class of Northwest Nazarene College (now a university) gathers on commencement day. In the front row: Margaret (Parsons) Koolhof, Mildren Sorensen, Laura Gates, Dr. Olive Winchester, Dr. R.V. DeLong, Ethel Allison, Alice Gronewald, Thelma Patterson. Mascot Johnny Sutherland is in front. In the back row: George Taylorson, Thor Gundmondson, Carl Falk, Letice Mylander, Ray Miller, Olive Miller, Bob Coulter, Harold Miller, Roscoe Hohn, Lauren Seaman and Donald Schwab.
Photo submitted Margaret Koolhof of Nampa

Roosevelt School Band

Members of The Roosevelt School Band pose for this photo. Teacher Mr. Nell, can be seen on the left. His wife, wanting to make the band look more professional, fashioned the band's hats out of cardboard.
Photo submitted by Miriam Keim Albright of Nampa

Amalgamated Sugar Company Annual Picnic

There was a big turnout of employees and their families at the Amalgamated Sugar Company's union members picnic in Lakeview Park in September 1944. From sleepy children to dapper guys wearing neckties at the picnic, no one wanted to miss the annual event. *Photo submitted by Gladys Messer of Nampa*

The Amalgamated Sugar Factory

Even in 1909 the Amalgamated Sugar Factory was a prominent business and building in Nampa. The factory is one of the largest sugar beet processors in the country. The sugar beet has been one of the major crops in the Treasure Valley thanks to the irrigation system.

Photo submitted by Dan Braudrick of Nampa

Nampa City Bus Lines
Louise and Perl Phillips stand in front of one of the buses used in their company, the Nampa City Bus Lines in 1946. Perl started the company with only two buses, a new Ford and a used one. The buses ran 16 hours a day and routes were scheduled so the entire city was covered by the line. No passenger had to walk more than two blocks to catch a bus. At the height of the company, 24,000 people were riding the bus each month. Students from Northwest Nazarene University were often hired as bus drivers.
Photo submitted by Shirley Phillips of Nampa

Window Shopping
Elaine Rose and her son Gilbert Jr. take a springtime stroll in downtown Nampa in 1946.
Photo submitted by Leota and Gilbert Rose of Nampa

First Baptist Vacation Bible School
Some of the hundreds of children who flocked to the area's vacation Bible schools are pictured in 1945 at the First Baptist Church of Caldwell, which stood at Blaine and 10th. The summer sessions offered week-long activities, fun and Bible study.
Photo submitted by Ermal Bowers of Caldwell

Cheesecake

Eileen Gibbs poses for a cheesecake picture on Nov. 1, 1945, to send to her husband, Allen, who was stationed in Camp Kohler, Mo., during World War II. The writing on the back of the photo says: "She's all yours, Allen. What more could you ask for? I am not conceited, just in love."

Submitted by Eileen Dunlap of Nampa

The Home Front

Raymond and his nephew Dale King of Caldwell pose in their sailor suits circa 1946. Dale wears a suit made for him by his mother, Leota. Both Raymond and his brother, Hershel served in the Navy.

Photo submitted by Dale King of Caldwell

Across from Lakeview School

Robert Farrar, right, and his brother-in-law Jack Stewart stand in front of the old Lakeview School in the 1940s. Farrar was born Oct. 15, 1909, and Stewart was born July 1, 1907. The Farrars' home was located right across from the school and you can see the school bell between the men. Farrar and his wife owned and operated several restaurants in Nampa until they retired in the 1980s.

Photo submitted by Bob Gibbs of Nampa

The Fred M. Hoadley Family

Fred and Phoebe Hoadley pose with their children, Eben, Eva Moon, Simon, Paul, Seth and Edith Skelton to mark their 50th wedding anniversary in 1943. The Hoadleys came from Kansas in 1909 and homesteaded in the Deer Flat Community. They farmed for 34 years before retiring.
Photo submitted by Homer Skelton of Caldwell

Van Buren's 6th Grade Class, 1949

Members of the Van Buren Elementary in Caldwell 6th grade class pose for a class photo in 1949. Van Buren is still located in Caldwell. Adults in the back are, left to right, Mr. Reed, teacher and Ralph Reid, principal. Back row: Darrell Mitchell, Betty Sue Dozier, Inez Lowe, Clifford Johnson, Vernon S., Bobby Hill, Florence Thornburg. Next row: Billy Kammeyer, Walter Berkenbile, Billy Wolford, Bonnie Lacy, Alice Witzig, Harold Dawson, Bobby S. Next row: Barbara Wagner, Lois Isaacson, Alvin Carr, Bernard Friend, David J., Harold Grove, Wendell Friend. Next row: George Frenier, Orvella Meek, Juanita ?, Jenetta Furnish, Betty Mager, Dorene Hale, Robert Taylor, Don Pasley. Front row: Clyde Holland, Owen Ogden, Marvie Thomas, unknown, Nellie Smith, Jennie Geer, Don Deitrick, Wayne King.
Photo submitted by Alice Witzig-Smith of Caldwell

In a Field of Clover

Seth Hoadley stands in a clover field in the late 1940s on the Wescott Farms, located on Malt Road south of Karcher. He rented approximately 100 acres on which he grew also potatoes, hay, grain, sugar beets, corn, peas and onions. He and wife Carrie raised eight daughters and two sons. Four are still living in the area, and grandson David Hoadley continues to farm the same ground.

Photo submitted by Shirley Oehler of Caldwell

Flour Mill Field Trip

The children in Nampa Lincoln Elementary's 3rd grade class pose proudly with one-pound bags of flour in 1953. They had taken a field trip to a flour mill on 2nd St. where Stone Lumber is now located. Included in the photo are: Jon Dobbs, Joyce Jenkins, Mary Beth Cox, Pam (Brant) Cunningham, Judy (Daniels) Gabriel, Lynn Chapman, Earl McCullough. Bill Zeckman, Dwight Reed, Dick Wilson, Terry Martin. BJ Morris, Ralph Filmore, Pam Lowe, Betty Jo Caldwell, and Sandra Manning.
Photo submitted by Jon Dobbs of Nampa

Living Christmas Tree

The children of the First United Presbyterian Church form a living Christmas tree for a holiday pageant in 1954. The picture was taken in the sanctuary of the church, which was at 15th Avenue South and 2nd Street in Nampa.
Photo submitted by Merrilyn King of Nampa

Jumping Rope

Ivey Games, Kathy Games, Gail Sperry, Gary Sperry (jumping rope), Marjorie Sperry, Howard Games and Everett Sperry gather in 1959 at the Games home in Notus after church on a hot summer Sunday for a picnic.
Photo submitted by Gail Gumaer of Caldwell

The Stringbuster Dance Band

The members of the Stringbuster Dance Band get ready for the filming of their weekly show on KBOI television. The band was the leading country western dance band in the area during the 1950s. They played at dance halls, the Seven Mile Dance Hall in Fruitland and in Caldwell. They also appeared on radio shows. Pictured, from left, are John Hall, Homer Davis, Delores Davis, Bill Hamby and Tom Rayne. Tom was known as the "barefoot hillbilly" when he was a disc jockey for KCID Radio in the early 1950s.
Photo submitted by Ardith Tepfer of Middleton

The Crew of International Harvester

The crew at the Caldwell International Harvester, located at 818 Main Street, pose for a photo taken in 1950. Standing in the back row, from left, Tom Morris, Filmore "Pappy" Morris, Pete Phillips, Crawford Otto, John Phillips, Fred Romjue, Carl Krebs, Unidell "Tex" Coles, Lew Dretke and Mike Kosmata. Front row, from left, Martin Ogren, Lou Savell, Jack Smith, John Mollerup, Johnny Grigg. Posing in the front row at far right is the International Harvester representative.
Submitted by Bonnie Vermass of Middleton

Owyhee Sheet Metal

Lloyd McLaughlin stands in front of his business, Owyhee Sheet Metal, in downtown Nampa in 1955. McLaughlin started the store in 1950, which was originally located in Homedale. He moved the business to Nampa in 1950. Lloyd's son Vic, along with partners Karla Woytach and Brent Erdly, purchased the store in 1988. The storefront was changed from the original facade when the company added True Value Hardware in 1965. Before Owyhee Sheet Metal moved in, Campbell Tractor and AT&T were located there.
Photo submitted by Audra McLaughlin of Nampa

Riding the Honey Wagon

Jim Longwill pulls his daughters, Darlyne and Lynda, on the "Honey Wagon" (the manure spreader). They are pictured on their farm in Middleton in 1953. *Submitted by Darlyne Alekcech of Marsing*

Helping Out

Almeda Gibbens, circa 1930s, helps drive the hay derrick on the family farm in Nampa. *Submitted by Faye Sturgis of Nampa*

The First Self-propelled Combine

This Allis Chalmers combine was the first-self-propelled combine owned by the Reineke family west of Melba around 1954.
Photo submitted by Luana Capps of Melba

Triplets!

What a threesome! Faye Sperry, left, and Marjorie Sperry tend to their rare triplet shorthorn heifers. The heifers were born in the spring of 1959 on their farm east of Notus.
Photo submitted by Gail Gumaer of Nampa

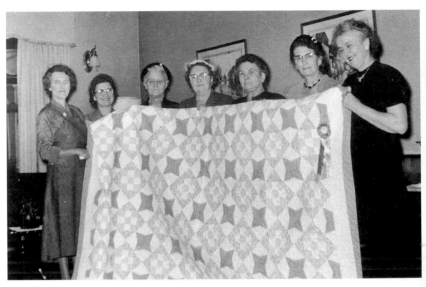

Nampa Valley Grange Quilters

The quilters of the Nampa Valley Grange hold up a quilt that was completed by the group circa 1950. Pictured are Anna Jones, Olive Hill, Eliza Woodman, Julia Ahrens, Jennie Duspins, Emma Wagers, and Mrs. Len Jordan, wife of the former governor.
Photo submitted by Roberta Witteman of Nampa

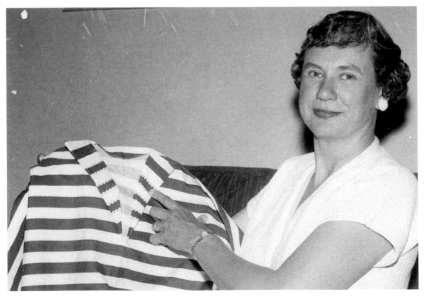

Sewing For the Miss Idaho Title

Irene Runkle of Nampa holds a blouse she made for the sewing portion of the 1958 Mrs. Idaho contest. She won the contest and was the runner-up in the Mrs. America competition.
Photo submitted by Irene Runkle of Nampa

Notus First Grade 1956

Students attending first grade at Notus Elementary pose for their class photo in 1956. Fifteen of the students were classmates through all 12 grades, graduating from Notus High School in 1968.
Photo submitted by Gail Gumaer of Caldwell

Spit the Bobcat

"Spit" the bobcat peers out from under a wooden structure in 1959. Spit was part of a unique zoo owned and operated by Clair Tepfer of Middleton from 1958 to 1961. The Middleton menagerie also included "Porky" the porcupine, chipmunks, raccoons, hamsters and many exotic birds. Tepfer closed his zoo and moved the animals to Boise when he became director of the Boise Zoo in 1971.
Photo submitted by Ardith Tepfer of Middleton

Truman's National Tour

President Harry Truman makes a stop in Nampa in 1950 during a national tour. Sheriff Ray Luekenga, wearing the white cowboy hat, can be seen in the bottom left corner of the photo. *Photo submitted by Dale Murphy of Nampa*

The Winter of 1950
Sox (John) Price of Wilder clears snow from a 10-day winter storm for the Boise Project Board of Control in 1950. The Highway Department did not have the equipment to clear the snow, so the board of control was sent out. *Photo submitted by John Dillon of Boise*

Flooding in Middleton
Lloyd Fluetsch gives baby Bette a close look at floodwaters on his farm near Middleton in 1956. Although not visible under all that water, the two are standing next to a canal.
Photo submitted by Bette Lee of Nampa

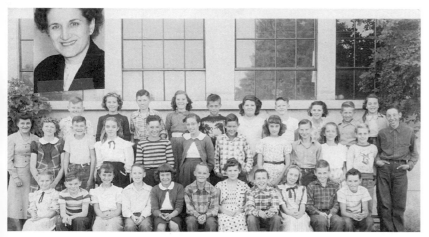

Mrs. Marshall's Class
Mrs. Madaline Marshall and her 1950 sixth grade Middleton class.
Submitted by Darlyne Alekcech of Marsing

Telephone Operators Reunion
Telephone operators from before 1937 gather in Nampa's Lakeview Park for a reunion in 1950. *Photo submitted by Janis Dunn of Nampa*

The Farm Bureau Insurance Agent
In April of 1949, Walter Higgins became the first Farm Bureau Insurance agent in Canyon County. Higgins continued to farm his 30 acres on the corner of Midway and Orchard in Nampa. At the time, horse and wagon insurance was still offered.
Photo submitted by Elsa Phelps of Nampa

Ready to Ride
Harry Doner Sr. gets ready to embark on one of his trademark rides around the Deer Flat area. Accompanied by various companions, Doner liked to visit his neighbors on horseback after retiring from farming.
Photo submitted by Roberta Witteman of Nampa

Nampa High School Band

Members of the Nampa High School Marching Band strut their stuff in a parade circa 1950. They are marching downtown near the intersection of 1st Street and 12th Avenue. *Photo submitted by Leota and Gilbert Rose of Boise*

Queen Darlyne

Queen Darlyne Longwill and Ken Bort tour Canyon County with the Snake River Stampede Caravan in 1955. The caravan traveled from town to town promoting the rodeo with singers who performed and led the crowd in cheers. *Photo submitted by Darlyne Alekcech of Marsing*

A.E. Ware Agency's New Office

Glen Reed, standing left, and A.E. Ware, standing right, look over the new office of the A.E. Ware Agency,, located at 112 3th Ave. S. in Nampa. Reed bought the agency from Ware in 1948 and made the move in 1950. Reed sold the agency to W.W. (Bill) Deal in 1982. *Photo submitted by Lillie Reed of Nampa*

Apple Box Racer

Ernie Dunlap sits in an apple box race car on Aug. 11, 1955, in front of his house in Nampa. The car was built by his brother Tommy, far left. Kitty Gibbs, center, stands behind the car that Tommy raced in Boise. *Photo submitted by Eileen Dunlap*

Mowing the Lawn

Thurman Boston mows the lawn with the help of his nephew, Mike Boston, left, and his daughter, Debbie in the early 1950s. The Boston home was on Smith Avenue in Nampa.
Photo submitted by Carol Boston of Nampa

Wilder Camp Crew

The Wilder Camp crew for the Boise project Board of Control takes a break to pose for a picture in the winter of 1953. From left: Clyde Jones; Alvie Mowery; Ray Kenyon; Marion Mattingly; Gene Hamons; and Cecil Hamons. *Photo submitted by John Dillon of Boise*

133

Safety Parade

With bikes decorated and flags flying, Girl Scout Troop 3 members make a colorful group for the Montgomery Ward Safety Parade in June 1950 in Nampa. The girls are, from left, Wanda Messer, Yvonne Brucks, Esther Berington, Elaine Coffman, Kathleen Wilske, JoAnn La Lande, Patricia Murray, Joyce Decker, Betty Johnson and Luann Little.
Photo submitted by Gladys Messer of Nampa

Treasure Valley Pigeon Club

The Treasure Valley Pigeon Club, formed by Clair and Ardith Tepfer, poses for a portrait in 1958. The Tepfers took this group of boys on several trips including competitions in Washington and the Grand Nationals in California. The club is still active in the Treasure Valley. From left: Trennis Blanc, Jackie Winters, Ardith Tepfer, Clair Tepfer, Curtis Cox and David Phillips.
Photo submitted by Ardith Tepfer of Middleton

Bringing in the Hay

The Stephens family brings in the hay on their
Middleton farm. Kathy and Wayne buck the bales as
Jim drives the tractor in this 1958 picture.
*Photo submitted by Kathy Gannussio and
Sonja Krave Stephens of Marsing*

The Federal Land Bank

Ray McClanham, father of Nampa resident Jean Fisher,
was the president of the Federal Land Bank in Nampa at
the time of this photo taken in 1957.
Photo submitted by Jean Fisher of Eugene, Ore.

Gene Autrey

Cowboy Gene Autry stands with nursing staff at Mercy hospital in 1950. The well-known actor and singer was the guest star of the Snake River Stampede that year. *Photo courtesy of Denise Jones, Mercy Medical Center, Nampa*

Time to Go

Clarence King, standing, takes his grandson Jerry and a friend for a ride in his covered wagon in 1950. Many Caldwell residents will remember King riding in this wagon, behind his two horses, Sadie and Sam, in the Caldwell Night Rodeo Parade.
Photo submitted by Dale King of Caldwell

A Buggy Ride

Earl and Opal Crooks ride in a buggy pulled by their horse, Blue, in Nampa in the late 1950s. *Photo submitted by Louis Reichart of Nampa*

Hat Parade

Members of the Bowmont Grange model their funny hats in a 1950 grange "hat parade." Pictured are: front row: Edgar Emmert, Mickey Reiniger, George Martineau and James Emmert; back row: Junior Martineau, Bob Marek and Eldon Gross.
Photo submitted by Roberta Witteman of Nampa

On the Oswald Homestead

LaVonna, Kerry, Leota, Bill and Jim Oswald play on the family homestead at the Black Canyon Project in 1955. The project included construction of a dam and formation of Black Canyon Reservoir that supplied irrigation water for transforming a large portion of desert into productive farmland.
Photo submitted by Leota and Gilbert Rose of Boise

Backbreaking Work

Farmworkers pick potatoes on the Miller farm outside Nampa, around 1954. Picking potatoes was backbreaking work in the hot sun. *Photo submitted by Dorothy Miller of Nampa*

Jefferson Junior High Cougar Band

Members of the Jefferson Junior High School "Cougar" Band in Caldwell pose for a group photo in 1955. Members of the band included: John Towery, trumpet; Joan Transue, bassoon; Kathy Ingram, sax; Judy Smith, horn; Stephen Clark, horn; John Walradt, baritone; Betty McCluskey, flute; Bonnie Mollerup, flute; John Wall, trombone; Jackie Kennedy, clarinet; David Bell, snare drum; Leland Thames, snare drum. *Photo submitted by Bonnie Vermass of Middleton*

Back in 1883
Banking in the good old days. Employees of the First National Bank (now Wells Fargo) in Caldwell pose in their 1883 costumes as they celebrate Caldwell's 70th year as a city. The photo was taken May 7, 1953. Seated in the front row are, from left, Ina Vokes, Wanda Clausen, Laura Tuning, Sylvia Hixson, Lola Layden, Vel Donna Lappin, Beth Johnson and Ms. Moore. The men in their derby hats are Stan Young, Ernie Ellingson, Bob Price, Lowell Jeffries, Bill Bethel, Joe Sellers, Jerry Miller, Ervin Cloud and E.K. Tunison.
Photo submitted by Sylvia Lawrence of Nampa

Edmark and the JayCees
Dave Edmark Sr. donates to a local fundraiser, at the urging of some attractive JayCees.
Photo submitted by Dave Edmark Jr. of Nampa

Posing with Buck
Lana Krajnik poses with her horse, Buck, just before riding in the 1959 Snake River Rodeo Parade in Nampa.
Photo submitted by Orveta Krajnik of Nampa

Gene Autrey and the Queen
Cowboy, movie star and Western singer Gene Autry stands with Snake River Stampede Queen Doris Tyson and members of the Beta Sigma Phi in 1950. Autry was the guest star of the Stampede that year. Other women in the picture are Irene Taylor, Ruth Yoder, Verla Tollifson, Dorothy Cambell and Dorothy Wander.
Photo submitted by Rosie Millward of Nampa

Confirmation
The first confirmation class from Trinity Lutheran in Nampa kneels at the altar in 1950. Pictured from left are: Freda and Elsa Higgins, Karleen Kock, Leroy Samuelson, Lewis Warner and James Kruger. Pastor Elmore Carlson stands. The church was located at 10th Ave. and 2nd St. S. in Nampa.
Photo submitted by Elsa Phelps of Caldwell

The Boy Who Would Play King
Around 1953, 3-year-old David Mangum rides his hobby horse in the garage of his Nampa home. Bronco Dave seems to believe that if you sit in the saddle "just so" and hang out your tongue, you can ride faster. Mangum grew up to be a teacher and to portray Jesus in the Easter pageant, "No Greater Love," at the First Church of the Nazarene for more than 20 years.
Photo submitted by Pat VanOrder of Nampa

Mr. Links' class
Mr. Links, far left, poses with his 1953-1954 fifth and sixth grade class at Lincoln School in Caldwell.
Submitted by Bonnie Vermass of Middleton

East Side School Football Team
The East Side School football team, complete with helmets and padding, marches in the Industrial Parade in downtown Nampa on Sept. 21, 1950. Marvin Messer is carrying the football in the front row.
Photo submitted by Gladys Messer of Nampa

First Day of School

Wilder Elementary students gather together for a photo in their neighborhood the morning of the first day of school in 1950. Front row: Linda Swigert, Linda Price, Marilyn Dobbins, Carl Dobbins, Bob Price. Back row: Sue Dobbins, Polly Price.
Photo submitted by John Dillon of Boise

Arbor Day with the Mayor

Sheryl Pedigo looks on with Nampa Mayor Preston Cappell and her Girl Scout troop as a tree is planted in Lincoln Park in 1955 in honor of Arbor Day. *Photo submitted by Sheryl Pedigo-Spinden of Nampa*

Lake Lowell Regatta

Art Godfrey gets ready for the 11th annual Lake Lowell regatta in 1955. He came close to the world record many times during his racing career. Art was one of the most consistent winners in the Northwest. For this race, he entered the F hydroplane and the F racing runabout divisions.
Photo submitted by Sheryl Pedigo-Spinden of Nampa

Huston Community Club

The members of the Huston Community Club pose for a picture in 1951. The club was formed on May 9, 1909, as the Ladies Aid Society of the Christian Church of the Deer Flat Community with 14 members. In 1925 it became the Huston Ladies Aid, and in 1928 it finally became the Huston Community Club. The club started the hot lunch program in Huston School in 1945. It also gave donations to various organizations and helped with local needs, such as burn outs, impoverished families and the Idaho State School and Hospital in Nampa.

Photo submitted by Jane Scroggins of Caldwell

Pete's Tavern

Pete's Tavern is a downtown Nampa fixture. The sign was installed in 1945 and is still hanging on the building.
Photo submitted by Gary Barr of Nampa

"I'll Meet You at the Phillips 66"

In 1952, the Phillips 66 filling station on the corner of North Kimball and the Highway was the center of activity at night in Caldwell according to owner Bob Nicholes. Gasoline sold for less than 30 cents per gallon. The station was torn down in 1980.
Photo submitted by Bob Nicholes of Caldwell

Class of 1953
Members of Mercy Hospital Nursing School's class of 1953 pose for their class photo. The students lived in the nurses' dorm and worked for three years before earning their degrees. This was one of the last classes to graduate from the school, which closed not long afterward.
Photo submitted by Esther Harrison of Nampa

College of Idaho Board of Directors
J.R. Simplot presides over a meeting of the College of Idaho Board of Directors in this undated photo.
Photo submitted by Clarke "Crusty" Hamon of Nampa

Ten Davis Class
The 7th and 8th grade class at Ten Davis school, in the 1950's.
Photo submitted by Sue Smith of Caldwell

Old Fashioned Swimsuit

Bernice Schumate poses in a self-made "old-fashioned style" swim suit she made with material donated by the J.C. Penney's store in Nampa. Bernice worked in the men's department at the store.
Submitted by Lester and Ruth Allen

Recipes from the Kitchen

JR Simplot Company employees put together a "Recipes for the Kitchen" booklet in 1962. The five women were reassigned from their usual duties in the Caldwell trim room to assemble the booklet. Included in the picture are, from left, Iva Mae Price, Fern Flynn, Veta Stephens, Helen Patterson and an unknown woman.
Photo submitted by John Dillon of Boise

Caldwell Armory Groundbreaking

Idaho Gov. Robert Smiley helps with the groundbreaking of the new Caldwell Armory in 1962. The armory was located at the Calvary Barn in Caldwell. The new building was built for 300 men in two national guard units. *Photo submitted by Clarke "Crusty" Hamon of Nampa*

The Future Mayor of Nampa

Nampa city employees pose in 1966. From left: Alex Henkel, John Dieffenbach, Noami Hagood, Maxine Horn and Reva McDaniel. Horn became Nampa's mayor in the late 1990s.
Photo submitted by LaRue McKnight of Nampa

The First Idaho Woman in the United States Congress

Henry Boston stands next to Grace Pfost at the 1961 dedication ceremony of Boston Avenue, in honor of Henry. Grace was the first Idaho woman to be elected to the United States Congress. Grace was also a member of the Nampa Chamber of Commerce, the Soroptimist club, Business and Professional Women's Club, League of Women Voters, Woman's Century Club, the Idaho Young Democrats and a Canyon County treasurer.
Photo submitted by Carol Boston of Nampa

Boots and Bows

Members of the Boots and Bows Square Dance Club pose in 1963 for a group picture in the special "play room" added to the side of their house by Penny and Ross Crispino so the group would have a place to dance. The club met Thursday nights and performed in downtown Nampa during Rodeo Week and on floats during parades. *Photo submitted by Edward Mower of Nampa*

Hay Stacking on the Miller Farm
Gus Miller uses farm machinery to stack hay on his farm east of Nampa in 1969. *Photo submitted by Dorothy Miller of Nampa*

On Chocolate Chip
Everett Sperry, grandson Cory and trusty steed Chocolate Chip prepare to spend the day working on the family farm east of Notus in 1969. The family raised silage corn, hay and sugar beets on their 80-acre farm. *Photo submitted by Gail Gumaer of Caldwell*

Keystone Cops
The Keystone Cops of the Caldwell Lions Club raise money for the March of Dimes by stopping traffic and soliciting donations in 1962. Pictured are: Joe Berenter, Pete Hamon, Clarke "Custy" Hamon, and Mark Johansen.
Photo submitted by Clarke "Crusty" Hamon of Nampa

Glen Evans Rock Collection

Glen Evans of Caldwell, seated second from right, enjoys the room
that he had built in his home to display his rock collection. Glen and
Ruth Evans collected rocks, minerals and turned gems into jewelry.
This photo was taken in the 1960s. At about that time, Glen and Ruth
wanted to have their collection enjoyed by others, but they wanted it
kept at a safe place. They donated their collection — valued at
$500,000 at that time — to Albertson College of Idaho, where it can
be viewed today by appointment. In 1922, Ruth and Glen turned
their fishing hobby into a business after their fish flies became
popular. The Evans Fish Fly Co. was founded in Caldwell and was
successful enough that it was expanded six times before being sold
to the Gladding Corp. Ruth died in 1972 and Glen died four years
later. The two were remembered as "gem collecting fishermen."
Photo submitted by Clarke "Crusty" Hamon of Nampa

The Ken Bort Band

Earl Simmons, Steve Cotrell, Digger O'Dell, Joe O'Dell
and Ken Bort pose for a publicity photo in the KFXD Radio
studio in 1960. Under the name of the Ken Bort Band, they
played at dances around Canyon County and in Boise. They
also played on the radio.
Photo submitted by Orveta Krajnik of Nampa

Sunday Smiles
The kindergarten students of the Nampa First Church of the Nazarene Sunday school class show big grins in this 1966 photo. In the front row: Kelly Husarik, Dana Freeborn, unknown, Joe Vasquez, Brian Snyder, unknown, unknown. In the back row: Teacher's assistant Esther Burkheimer, Carlene Cogdill, unknown, Delia Sandoval, unknown, Corrie Dean, Ron Diehm, unknown and Teacher Esther Michaelis.
Photo submitted by Eldon and Nellie Snyder of Nampa

Aprons for the Fair

The Dixie 4-H Club members of Caldwell show off their first sewing project — aprons — for the 1961 Canyon County Fair. Pictured are, from left, Sharon Houston, Janette Perkins, Janelle Perkins, Mary Parks, unknown, Esther Wuth and Gail Sperry. The fair was held in what is now the Caldwell Municipal Park.
Photo submitted by Gail Gumaer of Caldwell

Canyon County's Drill Team

The Canyon County Drill Team in the 1950s was made up of women mainly in their 30s and 40s. They practiced in the Central Gymnasium in Nampa once a week for two hours the entire summer and into the fall until they performed for the Grange in November. The drill team leaders were Bessie Harrison and Myrtle Barney.
Photo submitted by Lester and Ruth Allen

Playing the Calliope

Dr. Richard Skyrm plays the calliope in the State Centennial Parade in Caldwell, 1963. Skyrm was a professor of music at the College of Idaho, where he eventually became head of the music department.
Photo submitted by Jeanne Hayman of Caldwell

Onions Anyone?

Herman Huff, center, his hired man, George, and son Richard, document their incredible yield from the 1954 onion harvest. Herman also grew sugar beets and he revolutionized the sugar beet industry when he invented the first rotary beet topper in 1958. Until then, all beets were topped by hand. Herman patented the invention, but continued to pursue farming, his true passion, running a diversified farm on which he also grew clover, grain and potatoes. *Photo submitted by Jodi Huff of Nampa*

Troop 126

Boy Scout Troop 126 is loaded with members in 1964. In the front row are: Jeff linc, Dale Lee, unknown, unknown, Dennis Rogers, Alan White. In the second row are: Elva Rogers, Den Mother; Phil White, Grant Leavitt, unknown, unknown, Del (Todd) Weech, Gary Brown, unknown, unknown, Marvin McDorman, Jewell. In the third row are: Mike Smith, Gary Noe, Philip Cram, Rick Friddle, Tony Bradshaw, Benny Kochenower, Gary Stokes, Mike Cram, Warren Wylie, Steve Fine. In the back row are: unknown, Tony Marek and Gloria Kochenower.
Photo submitted by Madge Wylie of Melba

Dr. Faylor

Dr. M.M. Faylor stands proudly in his new dental clinic in 1952. Located at the corner of 7th Avenue and 2nd Street South in Nampa, the 1,500-square-foot clinic cost $20,000 to build. Also moving into the clinic were Dr. M.W. Faylor (father) and Reid Faylor (second son), who was still in dental school at the time.
Photo submitted by Peggy Faylor of Nampa

A Second Grand Opening for Karcher Mall

Developer Harry Daum, third from the left, greets JC Penney officials Oct. 16, 1968, at the grand opening of the second phase of Karcher Mall's expansion.
Photo submitted by John Simonis of Nampa

Karcher Mall

In 1965, Karcher Mall was the first retail shopping complex of its kind to be built in Idaho. The mall was built in what was then considered "the country," and was built by Harry Daum on an alfalfa field at the corner of Nampa-Caldwell Blouevard and Karcher Road. This photo was taken July 8, 1968, to mark the mall's first expansion that included JC Penney, Idaho Department Store and Skagg's Drug Store. The mall tripled in size and 30 shops were added.
Photo submitted by John Simonis of Nampa

Canyon County Sheriff's Posse
John Mollerup, during his time as a Canyon County Sheriff's Posse member, carries the United States flag atop his horse in downtown Caldwell. *Submitted by Bonnie Vermass of Middleton*

BIBLIOGRAPHY

• Bird, Annie Laurie. *Boise, the Peace Valley.*
  Caldwell: Canyon County Historical Society, 1975, c1934

• Leppert, Elaine C. and Thurston, Lorene B. *Early Caldwell.*
  Caldwell: The Caldwell Committee for the Idaho State Centennial, c1990

• Clark, Lynda Campbell. *Nampa Idaho 1885-1985, A Journey of Discovery.*
  Nampa: Nampa Centennial Committee, 1985

• Clark, Lynda Campbell and Holm, Debra Nelson and Holm, Norman Larry.
  Nampa's People 1886-1986, Discovering Our Heritage.
  Nampa: Nampa Centennial Committee, c1986

"Canyon County, A Treasure of Land and Its People," was a labor of love, and to all those who helped in any way, we express our appreciation. Special effort was made to ensure accuracy of information accompanying these photographs. However, information written on the backs of photographs and dates recalled by contributors may not have been exact. For historical accuracy, we welcome corrected/additional information. It will be forwarded to the appropriate archives and museums. Please write the Idaho Press-Tribune, Marketing Department, P.O. Box 9399; Nampa, Idaho, 83652.

Early Caldwell
This view of Caldwell from Canyon Hill dates from the
early 1900s. The Canyon County Courthouse is at left.
Photo submitted by Alice Witzig-Smith of Caldwell.